Contents

SpringerBriefs in Criminology

Translational Criminology

For further volumes:
http://www.springer.com/series/11178

Evidence-based crime policy is not just about rigorously generating a strong supply of research; it also involves meeting the demands for research in practice and policy. Knowing "what works" in reducing crime or increasing justice, or knowing "what explains" through rigorous criminological testing still must be converted to meaningful forms and implemented with fidelity in order for practice to be receptive to research. But how does this actually happen?

An important concept in the field of evidence-based crime policy is translational criminology, or how, why, and under what conditions research is converted to, and used, in practice. This Springer Brief series on translational criminology brings to both the academe and criminal justice world examples of how research turns into practice and policy, and the challenges thereof. Each brief will be written by top scholars and/or practitioners in the field who will describe specific examples of how a body of research became practice (or didn't) and the lessons learned from the endeavor. Through these examples, we hope ideas can develop about carrying out (and also testing) research translation.

Peter Greenwood

Evidence-Based Practice in Juvenile Justice

Progress, Challenges, and Opportunities

 Springer

Peter Greenwood
Advancing Evidence-Based Practice
Agoura, CA
USA

ISSN 2194-6442   ISSN 2194-6450   (electronic)
ISBN 978-1-4614-8907-8   ISBN 978-1-4614-8908-5   (eBook)
DOI 10.1007/978-1-4614-8908-5
Springer New York Heidelberg Dordrecht London

Library of Congress Control Number: 2013947370

Springer is part of Springer Science+Business Media (www.springer.com)

Abstract

In 15 years, evidence-based practice in juvenile justice has moved from concept to full blown practice in a number of states which have used research-based principles and programs to completely reorganize their system for treating juveniles, reduced crime and recidivism, and saved money in the process. This Brief will describe the major players in this transformative process, and the particular role they play in moving research to practice.

Keywords Violence prevention • Evidence-based programs • Implementation • Juvenile justice • Juvenile corrections

Chapter 1
Introduction

It has been almost 15 years since the Blueprints for Violence Prevention program at the University of Colorado first identified 10 programs that met their rigorous standards for being called a proven model program. During this same period, economists developed cost-benefit models that allowed them to estimate, with a fair degree of accuracy, the likely costs and benefits that would result if these programs were adopted, in particular settings. These cost-benefit studies suggested that in most states, every dollar invested in one of the more effective programs would result in $7–10 in benefits to taxpayers, mostly in the form of reduced spending on prison construction and operations (Drake et al. 2009; Greenwood 2006).

If these facts are indeed accurate then one might think that every state would be in the process of revising their service delivery and case disposition processes to take advantage of the opportunity. In fact, a number of states have responded to this knowledge by taking explicit steps to facilitate the implementation of these proven programs, often as alternatives or replacements for their more traditional programming. They have screened the lists of evidence-based programs (EBPs) put forward by various groups and adopted their own list of proven programs they support. They have established special funding streams to support the launch of new EBPs. They have adopted common assessment instruments so that different localities can compare results.

Some of these states have even set up resource centers to provide technical assistance to local providers and to monitor their progress in implementing these programs. Some have established local "compacts" for sharing the expected savings in state prison costs with counties who cut their admission rates through the use of EBPs. Yet, many others have not taken any but the most rudimentary steps toward embracing this new opportunity in the field of delinquency prevention.

Although the arguments in favor of shifting resources to evidence-based practice may sound compelling, the obstacles can be substantial. The first is financial. Prevention programs require coordinated local investment and action involving: juvenile courts, probation, mental health, public health, child welfare, education, and other stakeholders. Most of the direct financial benefits accrue to the state in

P. Greenwood, *Evidence-Based Practice in Juvenile Justice*,
SpringerBriefs in Translational Criminology, DOI: 10.1007/978-1-4614-8908-5_1,
© The Author(s) 2014

the form of reduced future prison commitments. In states where the juvenile court and probation are run by the state, this may not be a problem. But in the majority of states where juvenile courts, probation, and other social services are funded on a county basis, this will be a big problem until states devise some method of sharing the estimated savings with counties.

A second obstacle to reform is that non-evidence-based, programs may have developed strong political ties or local community support that make it difficult to close down. For many years now, connections to political leaders and the ability to withstand changes in administrations has been the hallmark of successful community based programs, not the quality of their services.

A third obstacle is the complexity of the coordination and implementation process that is required, which can take up to 2 years or more, and necessitates the active involvement of many key stakeholders. Many agencies have not had the experience of attempting to implementing any program with a high degree of fidelity.

Some communities get steered away from adopting some of the more complex models because the trainers of these models do not believe there is sufficient local support or administrative infrastructure to support their models. In addition, even when stakeholders and support are garnered, inevitable turnover in organizations means that the foundations built can be tenuous.

One final obstacle may be some confusion between best practice for juveniles and adults. In some jurisdictions, such as California, under so-called realignment legislation, local community corrections programs are being overwhelmed by their need to serve increased numbers of more serious adult offenders who can no longer be sent to prison. Some local agencies in these states appear to believe that the principles that guide community corrections are appropriate for guiding juvenile programming as well. Fortunately, these are all problems for which there are solutions.

This brief describes the strategies adopted by a number of states to increase the use of evidence-based programs being provided to at-risk youth and families. The next chapter reviews the coverage and reliability of the evidence base for juvenile justice programs and policies. Chapter 3 compares the progress of the states, and identifies some common steps that each of the leading states has taken to get where they are with respect to evidence-based practices. The following sections describe the specific paths that particular states have followed in regard to evidence-based programs for juveniles. The final section summarizes the lessons that these state studies can provide to those following in their path.

Chapter 2
Overview of the Evidence

2.1 Evidence-Based Programs

For anyone in a position to decide which programs should be continued or enhanced, which should be discontinued, and which new programs should be adopted, the issue should eventually come down to cost and effectiveness. Key questions include: What will specific programs cost to implement or continue in this specific setting? Are we prepared to implement such programs? How effective will they be with the population we have in mind? Do we have the infrastructure to support them? Answers to these questions now come in three distinct categories: brand name, generic, and principles.

Brand name programs include models such as Functional Family Therapy (FFT) (Alexander and Sexton 2002), Multi-Systemic Therapy (MST) (Henggeler et al. 1998), Multi-Dimensional Treatment Foster Care (MTFC) (Chamberlain and Reid 1998), and Nurse-Family Partnership (NFP) (Olds 2007). These are programs that were developed by a single investigator or team over a number of years and have been proven effective through repeated experimental trials, often supported by millions of dollars in federal grants. Brand name programs have met the selection criteria established by various review groups for identifying proven programs.

The generics are generalized strategies that have been tried by various investigators in different settings. Counseling, intensive supervision, and cognitive behavioral therapy all fall into this category. Generic methods are identified by meta-analysis and represent the efforts of independent researchers, each testing particular versions of the method.

The third category of what works includes a number of principles that have been found to apply across a variety of strategies. Principles are not programs per se, but techniques or approaches that have proven successful in reducing delinquency. For example, research has shown that focusing on the higher-risk offenders has the most impact on recidivism (Andrews and Dowden 2006), and increasing fidelity to exemplary models advances positive outcomes (Landenberger and Lipsey 2005).

P. Greenwood, *Evidence-Based Practice in Juvenile Justice*,
SpringerBriefs in Translational Criminology, DOI: 10.1007/978-1-4614-8908-5_2,
© The Author(s) 2014

There are so many lists of what works currently in circulation that one cannot avoid a decision about which to use. There are currently four reliable sources of information regarding effectiveness for delinquency prevention programs that can be combined to provide all the relevant information needed to make intelligent programming choices: (1) Blueprints for Violence Prevention; (2) meta-analyses conducted by Mark Lipsey; (3) publications by the Washington State Institute for Public Policy (WSIPP); and (4) the international Campbell Collaboration and its Crime and Justice Group's electronic library of systematic reviews, which covers a broader range of topics on crime and justice. These sources stand out because they employ a rigorous scientific standard of evaluation, are comprehensive, and are updated periodically.

The Blueprints list was developed by a research team, headed by Delbert Elliott, at the Center for the Study and Prevention of Violence, at the University of Colorado (Elliott 1997). For Blueprints to certify a brand name program as proven ("model"), the program must: (1) demonstrate its effects on targeted problem behaviors with a rigorous experimental design; (2) show that its effects persist after youths leave the program; and (3) be successfully replicated at least once. In order for a brand name program to be certified as "promising", the program must only demonstrate effects using a rigorous experimental design at one site.

The current Blueprints website (http://www.colorado.edu/cspv/blueprints) lists 11 "model" programs and 19 promising programs that were identified from a review of over 800 programs. These 11 proven programs include some that target drug use (Life Skills Training, Project Towards No Drug Abuse and the Midwestern Prevention Project); some that target very early behavioral problems (Nurse Family Partnership and the Incredible Years); some that target disruptive school behavior (Promoting Alternative Thinking Strategies, Bullying Prevention Program and Parent, Teacher, and Child Training Series); some that are preventive (Big Brothers Big Sisters of America Mentoring); and some were developed to deal with more serious delinquency (Multisystemic Therapy, Functional Family therapy, Multidimensional Treatment Foster Care).

Many of these programs target school-aged youths, in their classrooms or at home, before they are involved in the juvenile justice system. FFT, MST and MTFC are the three Blueprint models most frequently used with juvenile justice populations. These cost effective programs emphasize family interactions, probably because they focus on providing skills to the adults who are in the best position to supervise and train the child. Functional Family Therapy (FFT) targets youths aged 11–18 facing problems with delinquency, substance abuse, or violence. The program focuses on altering interactions between family members and seeks to improve the functioning of the family unit by increasing family problem-solving skills, enhancing emotional connections, and strengthening parents' ability to provide appropriate structure, guidance, and limits for their children (Alexander, Pugh, and Parsons 1998). It is a relatively short-term program (12–16 sessions over 3–4 months) that is delivered by specially trained therapists, usually in the home setting. Each team of four to eight therapists works under the direct supervision and monitoring of several more experienced therapist and trainers. The program is well documented and readily transportable.

Multisystemic Therapy (MST), also a family-based program, is designed to help parents deal effectively with their youth's behavior problems, including engaging with deviant peers and poor school performance. To accomplish family empowerment, MST also addresses barriers to effective parenting and helps family members build an indigenous social support network. To increase family collaboration and generalize treatment, MST is typically provided in the home, school, and other community locations. Master level counselors provide fifty hours of face-to-face contact over four months (Henngeler 1998). MST works with an individual family for as long a period as FFT does, but it is more intensive and more expensive. In addition to working with parents, MST will locate and attempt to involve other family members, teachers, school administrators, and other adults in supervising the youths.

For youths who have traditionally been placed in group homes—homes that are usually licensed to care for six or more youths who need to be removed from their home for an extended period, but do not pose a serious risk to themselves or others—the preferred alternative is Multidimensional Treatment Foster Care (MTFC). In MTFC, community families are recruited and trained to take one youth at a time into their homes. MTFC parents are paid a much higher rate than regular foster parents, but have additional responsibilities. One parent, for example, must be at home whenever the child is. Parent training emphasizes behavior management methods to provide youths with a structure and therapeutic living environment. After completing a pre-service training, MTFC parents attend a weekly group meeting run by a case manager for ongoing supervision. Supervision and support are also provided to MTFC parents during daily telephone calls. Family therapy is also provided for biological families. Random assignment evaluations find that arrest rates fall more among participants in the MFTC model than among youths in traditional group homes (Chamberlain 1998). Although it costs approximately $7,000 more per youth to support MFTC than a group home, the Washington State Institute for Public Policy estimates that MFTC produces $33,000 in criminal justice system savings and $52,000 in benefits to potential crime victims. The cost to support a single team for any of these models is approximately $500,000 per year. Depending on the model a single team can handle 40 (MTFC) to 160 (FFT) cases per year.

Meta-analysis is another approach to identifying the critical ingredients of effective programs. Mark Lipsey carried out the first meta-analysis that focused specifically on juvenile justice. In the most basic terms, a meta-analysis combines the results of independent studies with a shared research focus in order to analyze an overall effect, specifically called an effect size. Accordingly, Lipsey's analysis did not identify specific programs but did begin to identify specific strategies and methods that were more likely to be effective than others. Lipsey continued to expand and refine this work to include additional studies and many additional characteristics of each study (see Lipsey 2006, 2009; Lipsey and Cullen 2007). Based on the research he found that effective programs and strategies were those that were implemented well and targeted on high-risk offenders. He also found that strategies with a therapeutic component, such as counseling or skill building, are more effective than those with a control component, such as surveillance and discipline (Lipsey 2009). Although various forms of *cognitive behavioral therapy* (CBT) and *aggression replacement training* (ART) appear to be the most popular generic models, at this time there is no readily available data on how much effort states devote to these programs.

In order to help practitioners improve the effectiveness of their programs, Lipsey and his colleagues (Lipsey 2008; Lipsey et al. 2007; see also Lipsey et al. 2010) developed the Standardized Program Evaluation Protocol (SPEP), a hands-on tool that allows practitioners to compare programs operating in their local jurisdiction with what the research shows to be the most important factors associated with effectiveness. Each of the factors found in the meta-analysis to be importantly related to program effectiveness is represented in the SPEP and associated with a certain maximum number of points to provide a score. The number of points associated with each factor is derived directly from the statistical models used in the meta-analysis to predict program effects on recidivism. Those factors with stronger predictive relationships are assigned proportionately more points than those with relationships that are not as strong. Where appropriate, target values are set based on the median values found in the corresponding research, e.g., for service duration and number of contact hours.

SPEP is based on four key factors associated with program effectiveness: program type (primary and supplemental services); treatment dosage; treatment quality; and youth risk level.[1] Program type is considered the most important factor, with a possible 40 points out of a maximum score of 100. In addition to being designed to evaluate the overall effectiveness of individual programs against an "evidence-based practice profile" (i.e., the meta-analysis results), the SPEP can also inform practitioners about what program areas are in need of improvement. In this respect, it also acts as a process evaluation or monitoring tool, allowing practitioners to make adjustments that can improve effectiveness.

The Washington State Institute for Public Policy (WSIPP) uses meta-analysis methodology to conduct evaluations of both brand name and generic programs, but also considers the cost of such programs to taxpayers and crime victims, and weighs these costs against estimated benefits. Programs and strategies are not ranked, but effects on recidivism are measured and the number of evaluations is reported. Recidivism, cost to taxpayers and crime victims, and benefits are estimated using data specific to Washington State. The best feature of WSIPP cost benefit work is that compares the compares the cost effectiveness of different programs across government sectors. For instance the estimated Benefit/Cost Ration for juvenile justice programs is 21.6 for FFT, 41.7 for ART in institutions and 4.4 for MST. Investments in EBP for adult offenders yield Benefit/Cost rations of

---

[1] More detailed information on the application of the scoring system of these four factors is available from Lipsey et al. (2010, pp. 30-32).

19.0 for education in prison and 14.5 for alternative sentencing for drug offenders. Investments in substance abuse programs yield 44.4 for Motivational Interviewing with Motivational Enhancement for alcohol and 37.5 for Life Skills Training (Lee et al. 2012).

Established in 2000, the Campbell Collaboration is named after the influential experimental psychologist Donald Campbell (see Campbell 1969). Following the example of the international Cochrane Collaboration in medicine, the Campbell Collaboration aims to prepare systematic reviews (incorporating meta-analyses) of high-quality research evidence about what works in education, social work and welfare, and crime and justice. The Crime and Justice Group, consisting of 18 members from 11 countries, oversees the preparation and maintenance of systematic reviews of the highest quality research on the effects of criminological interventions and makes them accessible electronically to practitioners, policymakers, scholars, and the general public. As of this writing, the Crime and Justice Group had 32 published systematic reviews, and a number of these have already been updated. Many concern child development and juvenile justice, including parent training, school-based bullying prevention, mentoring, and cognitive behavioral therapy for offenders (Welsh and Farrington 2011). All published reviews are available at the Crime and Justice Group website (www.campbellcollaboration.org/reviews_crime_justice/index.php).

The programs and strategies identified by these four sources represent different types of challenges for jurisdictions when selecting programs. The proven Blueprints programs are all supported by developers with a wealth of experience, training, and technical assistance in implementation and sustainability. FFT and MST have been implemented in well over 200 and 400 sites, respectively (http://fftinc.com; http://mstservices.com). Well coordinated systems of program monitoring and oversight help ensure that client communities are receiving the outcomes they expect. In fact, it would be inappropriate for a provider to claim they were offering these programs without a direct and sustained linkage to the program developer. For generic programs identified by meta-analysis, potential adopters must first decide which specific model to adopt, based on its design, documentation, demands on an adopting agency, and the availability of technical assistance.

2.2 Implementation Science

The process of implementing evidence-based programs is on the way to becoming a science itself (Fixsen et al. 2009). The literature is clear that implementation is a process that takes 2-4 years to complete in most provider organizations. There are at least 6 functional stages of implementation, including: exploration, installation, initial implementation, full implementation, innovation, and sustainability (Fixsen et al. 2009). The stages are not linear as each impacts the others in complex ways. For example, sustainability factors are very much a part of exploration and full implementation directly impacts sustainability.

The goal of implementation is to have practitioners (e.g., foster parents, caseworkers, therapists, teachers, physicians) use innovations effectively. Based on the commonalities among successfully implemented programs across many fields, core implementation components have been identified (Fixsen et al. 2009). These components are staff selection, pre-service and in-service training, ongoing coaching and consultation, staff performance evaluation, decision support data systems, facilitative administrative supports, and system interventions. These interactive processes are integrated to maximize their influence on staff behavior and organizational functioning. The interactive core implementation components also compensate for one another in that a weakness in one component can be overcome by strengths in other components.

In the early days jurisdictions that were not fully prepared for the challenges that come along with the implementation of evidence-based programs would find themselves overwhelmed by staff turnover, complaints, and competition from other parts of the agency. By now, most of the developers of these proven programs, and the state level resource centers that work with them, have developed a much better sense of the infrastructure support that has to be in place before implementation can be successful. They have also become much better at coaching jurisdictions through the implementation process.

Chapter 3
State Progress Implementing Evidence-Based Programs

3.1 Availability of Evidence-Based Programs

As the goal of every state's efforts in regard to evidence-based practice ought to be to increase the use of these programs, it would seem that the appropriate outcome measure for these efforts is the number of proven model teams available, or the change in their availability over time.

When we want to measure prevalence of some characteristic or type of behavior within a population, such as homicide, drug use, or teen pregnancy, we usually specify the occurrences as a rate, say per 1,000 children or 100,000 population. Similarly, when we want to measure the availability of some health care service, such as CAT scans or pediatricians, we usually state their availability in terms of CAT scan machines or pediatricians per 100,000 population. This is to provide an "apples to apples" comparison in cases where the denominator varies from state to state. The availability of FFT, MST, or MTFC within any jurisdiction can similarly be measured in terms of the number of "therapist teams" available on a per capita basis.

For all three of these models, the team is the basic unit of operation, supervision, and training. Each team costs approximately $500,000 per year to support. Figure 3.1 shows the total number of FFT, MST, and MTFC teams per million population in each of the states that have at least one of the EBPs. Obviously there are great differences in their progress.

Figure 3.1 shows the number of family therapy teams per million population for all of the states that have begun to implement these programs. It is easy to see that there is a very wide spread between the top five states (Connecticut, Hawaii, Louisiana, Maine, and New Mexico) and all others. There is also a big difference between those in the middle range of progress and those who have made very little. The top five states share a number of characteristics in common. In all of them the administration of juvenile justice programs is completely separate from and not subservient to adult corrections and probation. In three of them juvenile justice is administered at the state level while Louisiana and Hawaii have local

P. Greenwood, *Evidence-Based Practice in Juvenile Justice*,
SpringerBriefs in Translational Criminology, DOI: 10.1007/978-1-4614-8908-5_3,
© The Author(s) 2014

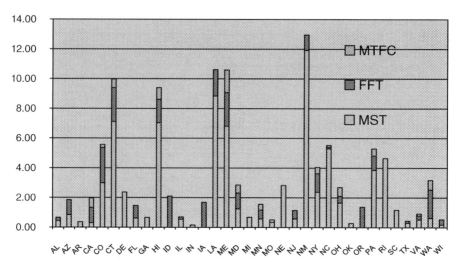

Fig. 3.1   Family therapy teams per million population, by state (Greenwood and Welsh 2012)

probation departments, which is typical of more than half the states in the nation. Four of the top five states started exploring EBPs in the late 1990s. Louisiana is the only one that did not begin.

Figure 3.2 shows the very same data but with the states sorted from those with the lowest number of teams to those with the highest. In New Mexico,

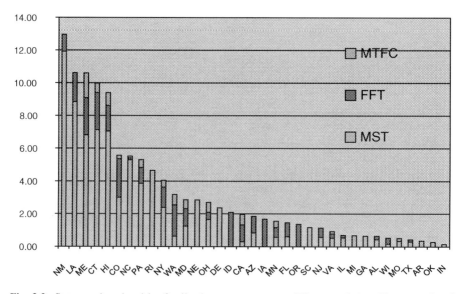

Fig. 3.2   States rank ordered by family therapy teams per million population (Greenwood and Welsh 2012)

Louisiana, Maine, Hawaii and Connecticut, with availability of these programs averaging more than 10 per million individuals in the population, program availability is more than double that in the four states with the next highest availability (Colorado, North Carolina, Pennsylvania, and Rhode Island). Figure 3.2 also shows that MST is the most available of these three family-focused proven model programs.

3.2   Commonalities Between Leading States

Other similarities that are a good indication of how other states should proceed include:

Turning crisis into opportunity: Three of the leading states were being sued by the federal Department of Justice over conditions in their juvenile institutions. In the other two there was a growing political consensus that many youth being sent to placement did not belong there. All five leading states were able to capitalize on this crisis of confidence by bringing appropriate stakeholders together and identifying capable individuals to take charge.

Structured involvement of all key stakeholders: Effective changes in juvenile justice programming efforts require the cooperation of many state and local agencies, including state departments of children and families, mental health, probation, law enforcement, and school systems. All of the leading states created high-level stakeholder groups to oversee the process of rolling out EBPs. In Connecticut it was the Governor's Blue Ribbon Commission on Mental Health in 2000; In Maine it was the Juvenile Justice Advisory Group; In New Mexico it was the Behavioral Health Collaborative; in Louisiana it was the Juvenile Justice Implementation Commission; and in Hawaii it was the EBS Task Force and the local Community Councils.

Emergence of champions: All of the five leading states had widely recognizable champions that varied from key department heads, to a behavioral health consultant, to the governor of one, to an associate commissioner of corrections in another. Everybody knew who these champions were, and they were effective in that role.

Development of local expertise: All of the leading states identified at least one person to become fully informed about the available EBP options and made the time available for them to do this, including travel to operational sites and training in specific models.

Pilot testing of new evidence-based programs: All but one of the leading states picked one or two sites in which to test the program models they had selected as the best to suit their needs. The pilot tests were closely monitored and the results were widely shared.

Creation of information resource centers: These centers, sometimes called the Center for Effective Practice (CEP), became the primary bridge between the science of EBP (e.g., review articles, assessment instruments, training consultants) and the practitioners. CEP staff would sit in on practitioner meetings to better understand their needs, and then develop analytical or informational tools to help address them. Practitioners would ask CEP staff for information about particular problems, or programs they may have heard about, and receive timely, unbiased answers.

Designation of small number of EBPs to be supported by state: All of our leading states started out supporting just one EBP, either MST or FFT, and all of them added additional programs to the list of what they supported, albeit slowly. NM and HI still mainly support MST, with just a few FFT teams currently in operation. Connecticut, while still a heavy MST user, has elected to support more than a half-dozen other proven or promising models.

Special funding for designated evidence-based programs: The availability of funds to support the very important but non-revenue producing pre-implementation aspects of a new EBP can be a challenge. That challenge is reduced if the state can support some of those costs.

Technical assistance to counties for needs assessment, program selection, and implementation: Since, in most states, counties are far from uniform in size or demographics, it is seldom likely that a one-size policy reform will fit all. Research has demonstrated that local communities will get better outcomes if they receive proper training in how to assess their needs, select programs, and then implement them. It has been proven that the spread of EBPs becomes much more rational and effective when states are able to serve local communities in this way (Hawkins et al. 2008).

Chapter 4
Connecticut and Hawaii: Early Starters With Quite Different Results

4.1 Connecticut

Connecticut is the third smallest state in terms of area, encompassing only 5,500 square miles or 0.15 % of the total US land mass. Its small size makes commuting to the state capital (Hartford) possible from any part of the state. Relatively, Connecticut is the fourth smallest state in the nation. It ranks 37th in terms of water area, with nearly 700 square miles (IPL 2012).

In total population the state ranks 29th, right between Oklahoma and Iowa. For other comparison purposes its population of 3.5 million is slightly less than the City of Los Angeles (4 million) and slightly more than San Diego County (3.1) million. The state is slightly below average with respect to juvenile population, with 5.7 % being under 5 and 22.9 under 18. Finally, Connecticut is just over the national average in terms of racial make-up, with 77.6 % of its population being white.

Juvenile Courts and programming are administered on a statewide basis in Connecticut, rather than by county, which is the case in many other states. Up until this year, the state was one of the few in which minors were still handled in adult criminal courts after their 16th birthday. In 2007, Connecticut's legislature raised the age of adult jurisdiction from 16 to 18, effective January 1, 2010. Except for serious and violent offenders, minors will be in the juvenile justice system. In fact, the campaign to raise the juvenile age limit in the state began about the same time that it began moving aggressively into EBP, and involved many of the same players.

4.1.1 Crisis of Confidence

The state Department of Children and Families DCF has four mandates: child welfare; behavioral health (including substance abuse); juvenile justice; and prevention. As in many other states, DCF had been confronted with serving many children and families with high levels of need who were using high levels of care, including inpatient

P. Greenwood, *Evidence-Based Practice in Juvenile Justice*,
SpringerBriefs in Translational Criminology, DOI: 10.1007/978-1-4614-8908-5_4,
© The Author(s) 2014

treatment and residential care. In 2000, the Child Health and Development Institute (CHDI), an independent policy and research institute, released a study entitled, "Financing Children's Behavioral Health Services in Connecticut" (Meyers 2000). The study showed that 70 % of the resources that Connecticut was devoting to children's mental health were being spent on a relatively small number of children who were receiving high levels of care, mostly out-of-state residential placements. The remaining 30 % of state resources were spent on the far greater number of children receiving community and home-based services.

As a result of that study, the state legislature and the Governor's Blue Ribbon Commission on Mental Health called for system reform (Franks 2010). By 2001, a variety of stakeholders from across the state worked with the state's legislature to pass sweeping children's mental health reform legislation entitled "Connecticut Community KidCare." This legislation called for a variety of reforms, including a "carve-out" of the state's behavioral health services, development of a statewide "system of care" model, an emphasis on family-driven, family—centered care, and a shift of resources to create more community-based services. A decrease in the number of children being sent to out-of-state residential facilities was observed in subsequent years (Franks 2010).

The strategy adopted by the state for creating more community-based services was to identify effective alternatives to residential treatment that could be delivered in the home or community. EBPs had by this time begun to emerge as an effective means of accomplishing this goal. Although the KidCare legislation was essentially an unfunded mandate, champions at DCF began to explore opportunities for shifting resources and identify new sources of funding to implement EBPs as alternatives to costly residential care. An additional impetus for state agencies to explore adopting EBPs came from the Connecticut Alcohol and Drug Policy Council on Juvenile Justice, which cited the importance of effective programs for this population of children and youth (Franks 2010). As a result of these factors, DCF was provided with funds from a federal Byrne Grant for an initial pilot program to implement Multisystemic Therapy (MST) for high-risk children and youth with substance abuse and behavioral problems (Henggeler and Lee 2003).

The first MST team was implemented in 1999 and its outcomes were monitored closely. When early indicators suggested that MST treatment was an effective alternative treatment for children and youth with substance abuse and behavioral disorders, and it allowed them to remain in their homes and communities, there was an increased interest in disseminating MST more widely (Franks 2010).

Given the early pilot's success and a desire to build and expand the program, Connecticut was confronted with the challenge of how to bring MST to scale within the state's system of care. DCF lacked the internal resources to be the "purveyor" of MST so turned to stakeholders within the system who had the expertise and mission to expand effective models of care. This resulted in the founding of the Connecticut Center for Effective Practice (CCEP) as a division of the CHDI. The Center was initially created as a partnership between an independent institute (CHDI), state agencies that serve children, and the state's major academic institutions with medical schools (Yale University and University of Connecticut). Early partners included the state's DCF; the Court Support Services Division of the Judicial Branch of Connecticut (CSSD); the University of Connecticut Health Center, Department of Psychiatry; and the Yale Child Study Center. As the Center developed over time and its work evolved, additional partners joined the Center, including the Consultation Center at Yale University and FAVOR, a statewide parent advocacy organization (Franks 2010).

Once established, CCEP helped disseminate MST across the state and implemented over 25 MST teams over a 5 year period between 2001–2006 (Franks Schroeder Connell and Tebes 2008). Initially, the Center worked closely with MST Services, Inc. to become a licensed systems supervisor, providing all the training, coaching, quality assurance, and outcome evaluation through collaboration with local and national partners. Over time, CCEP transitioned the quality assurance and systems supervision to another Connecticut-based organization, Advanced Behavioral Health, and used the experience to build its internal capacity and develop expertise in the dissemination of an EBP (Franks 2010).

In many ways, the dissemination of MST was an impetus for state agencies to invest in disseminating a range of other EBPs. CCEP has not been involved in all of these efforts, but the Center for Best Practices at CSSD and the Department of Behavioral Health at DCF have been involved in disseminating a range of other EBPs since MST, including FFT, MDFT, BSFT, MTFC, DBT, and a home grown in-home program known as IICAPS. In addition, CCEP in collaboration with DCF has been involved in the dissemination of TF-CBT and through support of the Robert Wood Johnson Foundation, another home-grown EBP, Child FIRST. So, in many ways the "success" of the state in disseminating and implementing a range of EBPs is really the result of progressive thinking at those state agencies that serve children.

4.1.2 Center for Best Practices (CBP)

This center was established by CSSD in 2001 after agency administrators took a trip to Canada and tapped into the rich literature on recidivism reduction that was being created there by Don Andrews, Paul Gendreau, and others. That trip was predicated on some anecdotal sense that CSSD's sizable network of contracted services was not achieving as much as it could. Initially, the CBP consisted of only two staff, one for adult probation programs and another for juvenile programs. The original two managers were pulled out of daily responsibilities and encouraged to read and hound EBP architects for as long as it took.

At about that time the legislature asked for an independent analysis of the Judicial Branch's appropriation for contracted services, which had gone from next to nothing for programming for juveniles in 1995 to nearly $20,000,000 by the early 2000s. The Connecticut Policy and Economic Council (CPEC) conducted an analysis that compared kids in CSSD and DCF programs to a matched sample of kids who received no services at all.

The study found that youths who were receiving services recidivated at a statistically significantly higher rate than their control group counterparts. These findings, and the attention they attracted, created the impetus for change and permitted the politically sweeping changes that followed. In a period of 9 months, CSSD terminated contracts totaling about $8 million, three homegrown program models that were available across the state, and reinvested most of the money in MST.

During this expansion phase, Peter Panzarella especially, and CCEP to some smaller extent, were extremely helpful in the rapid transition. So was MST Services, with whom CSSD established a contract for technical assistance. Essentially they had pretty much unlimited access to Dan Edwards, Marshall Swenson and Keller Strother, from MST Services, and called on them more than weekly (sometime at off hours) to plan and strategize implementation. According to Julie Revaz, it was a very steep learning curve.

For funding, CSSD generally used the same monies that had been spent on the ineffective models known as Juvenile Supervision and Reporting Center (JSRC), Intensive Outreach and Monitoring (IOM), and Gateway. These contracts were ended in four phases over 9 months and replaced with MST teams (15 in total) as the services were closed.

Currently, DCF holds the contract with Advanced Behavioral Health (ABH) for quality assurance, and CSSD provides money to them to support their share. The agencies co-manage the contract and have a collaborative approach to establishing benchmarks. CSSD has one employee, a Court Planner, who monitors the contracts, and who acts as a liaison between programs, probation and ABH. Senior staff are called in and participate in quarterly meetings as the "resident institutional memory" or for issues with greater complexity, interdisciplinary or inter-system involvement, exposure or historical roots.

Over time CEP added another manager whose focus is the unique needs of girls and women, as well as several Court Planners, who serve as professional support staff. The CBP has more than tripled in size, and is now responsible, within CSSD, for staying abreast of all research and literature reviews regarding recidivism reduction, recommending new programs or practices, consulting to Operations (probation) on their policies, shepherding new agendas, and early implementation (first 1–2 years) of new programs. Thereafter, as in the case of MST, they stay on as resources, advisors, and oft-times public speakers. Other staff "Monitors" ensure contract compliance, process budgets, deal with utilization, etc. Today CSSD funds MST, BSFT, FFT and some MDFT. DCF also has MTFC. Clearly, CT is deeply into the EBP business!

One of the things that Julie Revaz believes enabled her to be an effective Program Champion for MST back in the early days is having taken the 5 day training, read the book, taken the test, spoken to supporters and nay-sayers of the model, met with the Blueprints crew, observed consultations, rode around and sat in on sessions with therapists, attended Site Visits with probation, etc. She believes her successor in the program champion role, also made a great move in creating a document that chronicled decisions that were made along the way, and their rationale. He posted it so sites across the state could consult it when faced with new obstacles or opportunities.

In many ways the dissemination of MST was an impetus for state agencies to invest in disseminating a range of other EBPs. CCEP has not been involved in several of these efforts, but the Center for Best Practices at CSSD (Julie Revaz) and the Department of Behavioral Health at DCF (Bert Plant) have been involved in disseminating a range of other EBPs since MST including FFT, MDFT, BSFT, MTFC, DBT and a home grown in-home program, IICAPS. In addition, CCEP in collaboration with DCF has been involved in the dissemination of TF-CBT and through support of the Robert Wood Johnson Foundation, another home-grown EBP, Child FIRST. In many ways, the "success" of CT in disseminating and implementing a range of EBPs is really the result of progressive thinking at the state agencies that serve children. CCEP has been a partner in much of that work, but it would not be possible without the leadership and resource investment from the Department of Children and Families and the Judicial Branch. State agencies have really led the way in these efforts and should be celebrated as being both progressive and responsive to the needs of children and families in Connecticut.

Although the original goal of the Center was to disseminate MST across the state, founding partners saw an opportunity to create an entity with a much broader mandate. Early stakeholders anticipated that there would be a growing need to identify and implement best practice models of care and support the reforms being driven by Community KidCare. The Center's vision was thus established to: "enhance Connecticut's capacity to improve the effectiveness of treatment provided to all children with serious and complex emotional, behavioral and addictive disorders." Its mission was to: "develop, train, disseminate, evaluate and expand effective models of practice to improve the diagnosis and treatment of children with serious and complex mental health conditions in Connecticut" (Franks 2010).

In 2003, the Center published *Close to Home*, a report which described existing practices in the juvenile justice system and made recommendations to improve and enhance those services to better meet the behavioral health needs of children and families (Ford Gregory McKay and Williams 2003). This report served as a catalyst for many improvements in service delivery in the juvenile justice system [Note to PWG: you raise the question, "like what?"] and shifts towards more evidence-based, family-centered treatments (Franks 2010).

In 2005, the Center published a follow-up report, *Not Just Child's Play*, which focused on the role of screening and assessment in the juvenile justice system, identifying best practice models, and identifying gaps within the Connecticut system (Williams Ford et al. 2005). Like its predecessor, this report helped facilitate changes in the system, including how screening and risk assessment are utilized to help identify children's needs and match them with the most appropriate available services (Franks 2010).

Also in 2005, the Center further refined its mission by identifying a four-point framework for action:

1. Identification, adoption, and implementation of evidence-based and best practices.
2. Research, evaluation, and quality assurance of new and existing services.
3. Education and raising public awareness about evidence-based and best practices.
4. Development of infrastructure, systems, and mechanisms for implementation and sustainability (Franks 2010).

The Center For Effective Practice was initially funded by a start-up grant, with subsequent core funding from the Connecticut Health Foundation (CHF), a charitable conversion foundation based in Connecticut that includes mental health systems change as part of its mission. In addition, soon after the early start-up of the Center, Connecticut's DCF also provided a multi-year contract to support the operations of the Center, initially funding the dissemination of MST and providing core support for its broader mission (Franks 2010).

The DCF and CHF core funding, which once totaled about $500,000 per year, have both since ended, creating a challenge for the Center. However, a variety of successful bids for state contracts and other successful grant seeking efforts have sustained the Center over time. In addition, the parent foundation of CHDI (The Children's Fund of Connecticut), where the Center is housed, has increased its funding and support in recent years to partially address the gap resulting from the discontinuation of funding from state and foundation sources.

Despite these successes, in the absence of core funding, the Center is now dependent on bidding for available grants and contracts and is no longer able to proactively identify and address problems as it had in the past. This more formal relationship makes it difficult for the Center to problem solve or consult informally with its former partners without being disqualified as a possible bidder on any new work (Franks 2010).

4.1.3 Partnerships and Governance

The early vision for the Center was that it would be a partnership between the major academic institutions in the state (Yale University and University of Connecticut), state agencies serving children (DCF and CSSD), and a non-profit institute (CHDI), where core issues impacting children's mental health could be identified and analyzed to promote systems change. However, due to a changing economic climate, tighter restrictions in state contracting procedures, and challenges with identifying the capacity in the partner academic institutions to do the work, over time the Center began to function less as a partnership and more as an independent entity with its own internal capacity to achieve its vision and mission.

Initially, the Center was governed by a Steering Committee comprised of representatives from each of the partner institutions. This committee met on a monthly basis, provided oversight, and helped steer the direction of the Center and use of its resources. On an annual basis the board would identify and vote on strategic priorities that would be addressed over the next year. Over time, as staff gained expertise and built internal capacity, their reliance on affiliated academic institutions diminished and the Center acted more autonomously (Franks 2010).

4.1.4 Accomplishments

The Center for Effective Practice engaged in a range of activities which it distinguishes into seven main areas: (1) consultation activities; (2) best practice model development; (3) purveyor of EBPs; (4) quality assurance and improvement; (5)

outcome evaluation and research; (6) training, public awareness, and education; and (7) policy and systems development. These activities are conducted through two main mechanisms: internal capacity through expertise of the Center staff, and collaboration with external experts and resources. As the Center evolved over time and staff gained both experience and recognition with statewide stakeholders, the range of activities conducted by the Center has relied less on external expertise and more upon internal capacity (Franks 2010).

Some reports developed by the Center focused on areas of high need identified by state agency and academic partners. Reports focusing on youth suicide (Dore Aseltine Franks and Schultz 2006), and substance abuse and caregiver parenting and attachment (Tay 2005), were also developed to address challenges being confronted by the state's behavioral health system. Recently, the Center completed a report analyzing the state's outpatient system of care for children that is being utilized to promote system improvements and implementation of best practices (Vanderploeg Bracey and Franks 2010). These reports helped identify best practice models of care and made recommendations for enhancing and improving services at the policy, systems, and practice levels.

4.1.4.1 Best Practice Model Development

As DCF began to examine the effectiveness of behavioral health services in Connecticut, it turned to the Center to help identify best practice models of care. In the past 4 years the Center has developed best practice models of care for several different key services within the spectrum of care. CHDI worked with an external expert consultant to develop and identify a model of practice for therapeutic support services (often referred to as "therapeutic mentoring;" Davis 2007).

Similarly, the Center worked with DCF and one of its partner organizations, the Yale Consultation Center, to develop a best practice model for Extended Day Treatment (EDT) services (Vanderploeg Franks Plant, Cloud and Tebes 2009). This process included identifying established best practice models, interviewing and documenting the practice of existing EDT service providers in the state, and building recommendations on demonstrated successful practices. This effort led to an ongoing collaborative process among DCF, provider organizations, and the Center. This resulted in the implementation of new practice standards and improvements in the delivery system (Franks 2010).

The Center also was asked to develop a model of care for the EMPS program. EMPS is a mobile statewide service that is meant to relieve the burden on emergency departments and provide urgent assessment, triage, short-term treatment and referral for children in their community anywhere across the state. After a comprehensive process which involved identifying national best practice models of care, a series of interviews with expert researchers and consultants, analysis of the current services being delivered in Connecticut and identification of best practices that were currently being delivered, the Center developed a new model for this service which resulted in a major re-procurement and reorganization of these services across the state (Vanderploeg Schroeder and Franks 2007). "Despite initial resistance to these changes at the practice and policy levels, the changes in service delivery have been very successful with documented improvements in practice and outcomes" (Franks 2010).

Since the dissemination of MST, the state has invested and built capacity in providing a range of other in-home EBPs including, FFT, Multidimensional Family Therapy, Brief Strategic Family Therapy, and Multidimensional Treatment Foster Care. Because of the variety of in-home EBPs now available in the Connecticut system, the Center developed a decision making model to help state agencies and provider organizations make appropriate decisions regarding utilization of these services (Vanderploeg and Meyers 2009).

As it evolved, CCEP continued to act as a purveyor of other large-scale initiatives to disseminate evidence-based or promising practices across Connecticut. More recently, in the summer of 2010, the Center worked closely with DCF to complete a 3-year dissemination and implementation trial of Trauma-focused Cognitive Behavioral Therapy (TF-CBT; Cohen Mannarino and Deblinge 2006). Through funding from DCF, this established EBP was disseminated to 16 outpatient providers geographically distributed across the state to meet the needs of traumatized children and their families. The learning collaborative methodology, developed by the Institute for Healthcare Improvement and adapted by the National Center for Child Traumatic Stress at Duke University, was utilized as the mechanism to disseminate this EBP. The learning collaborative is proving to be a highly effective mechanism for disseminating EBPs as evidenced by both outcomes and practice changes across the state. This model has been embraced by the Center as a viable model for systems change that can be applied and adapted to other best practices within a large-scale system of care.

Currently the Center, through contracts with state agencies supported by a Substance Abuse and Mental Health Services Administration (SAMHSA) Mental Health Transformation State Incentive Grant is implementing the Wraparound Milwaukee model in two demonstration sites (one urban, one non-urban), to explore and establish the benefits of family-centered community-based care for children and families. Through collaboration with external experts from Wraparound Milwaukee and local academic, state, and family partners, the Center is acting as the coordinating center for the initiative, providing training, consultation, capacity building, coaching, and outcome evaluation of the Wraparound initiative in two communities. It is hoped that the outcomes of this initiative will inform system of care development across the State of Connecticut.

The Center is also providing consultation on the learning collaborative methodology and quality assurance technical assistance to help implement an emerging EBP, Child FIRST, across Connecticut. This early childhood parent-child home-based intervention was developed by a Connecticut developmental pediatrician and has been shown to have extremely promising outcomes for children and caregivers who receive these early intervention services. Through the support of a Robert Wood Johnson Foundation grant, the Center is working with the treatment developer to help disseminate the Child FIRST model to six agencies across the state over a 2-year period, to help establish an infrastructure to support this practice across Connecticut, and further build the early childhood system of care

(Franks 2010). The Center also engaged in a major research and outcome evaluation study of MST in Connecticut following its transition from system supervisor (Franks et al. 2008). In this instance, the Center shifted from the role of implementation to research and evaluation. This large-scale study examined not only MST outcome data, but also objective reports of recidivism, and established.

4.1.5 Quality Assurance and Improvement

An integral aspect of the Center's work as an intermediary organization is quality assurance and continuous quality improvement. In many of its initiatives the Center helps individual providers and state systems use metric and quality assurance data to monitor program fidelity, improve practice, and promote higher standards of care. This is evidenced in the Center's work on the TF-CBT initiative where it continues to collect, analyze and disseminate quality assurance data to provider organizations that have implemented the practice. In collaboration with DCF the Center has established a comprehensive system for continuous quality improvement. The Center is also working with the developers of Child FIRST to develop a similar system for quality assurance and improvement.

Another example of the role the Center plays in promoting quality is the Performance Improvement Center (PIC), which was established by DCF following the implementation of the recommendations for service improvement in the EMPS initiative (Vanderploeg et al. 2007). The PIC is housed at the Center and provides all training, technical assistance and continuous quality improvement services to providers of EMPS across the state. The PIC trains the provider organizations in core practice elements and collects data that examines quality and performance over multiple domains. This data is shared transparently across all providers and analyzed at the system and provider levels to help drive practice improvement (Franks 2010).

4.1.6 Training, Public Awareness, and Education

The Center engages in ongoing efforts to train and educate both professionals and consumers of behavioral health services, as well as academic and community partners. Center staff is also contacted by state agencies and other stakeholders to provide training on a wide range of topics from child and adolescent development to implementation of EBPs. As an integral part of CHDI, the Center also works to develop resources and materials to help educate professionals who deliver care to children across the state. In a variety of roles, the Center helps to promote workforce development and identification of capacities needed to implement quality care. The Center is also committed to working with its family partners to engage parents and caregivers and raise their awareness and create demand for effective services. Examples of this work include the development of a comprehensive guide to the juvenile justice system for families (Williams Franks and Dore 2008) and an extensive website recently launched to help parents and caregivers navigate the behavioral health system (www.kidsmentalhealth.info.com) (Franks 2010).

4.2 Hawaii

Evidence based family therapy came to Hawaii early in the twenty-first Century, as it did with 3 of the other 5 lead states, again with motivation provided by a consent decree, but with the other party being, youth who needed mental health services rather than those in the juvenile justice system. The early MST programs were part of a major reform of mental health services for adolescents based on evidence-based practices. With more than 10 teams per million population, involvement with MST is currently limited to youth refereed for mental health services, primarily by the schools, not by the juvenile court.

Hawaii is the 8th smallest state, the 11th-least populous, but the 13th-most densely populated of the 50 U.S. states. For juvenile justice, Hawaii is a combination state, meaning that delinquency services are organized at both the state and local level. Furthermore, responsibility is divided between the judicial and executive branches. Family Courts are responsible for secure detention, delinquency intake, predisposition investigation, and probation supervision. The Office of Youth Services, within the Department of Human Services, administers commitment programs and aftercare.

Juveniles who are first-time of-fenders or are charged with misdemeanors may be eligible for diversion projects or informal adjustment at the Family Court. There is no state mandated risk/needs assessment instrument used to determine levels of probation supervision. The Youth Level of Service/Case Management Inventory is used to identify juveniles' service needs and to measure their risk of recidivism when considering placement options (as of 2005).

4.2.1 EBP Comes to the Islands

Two separate movements brought EBPs in the form of MST, and then FFT, to Hawaii. One was a federal court decree requiring the state to provide improved services and programs for all disabled youth. The other was new and energetic leadership in the Child and Adolescent Mental Health Division of the Department of Health

Parents of several disabled children filed a class-action lawsuit in 1993, alleging that the State of Hawaii was violating the federal **Individuals with Disabilities in Education Act** because it failed to provide mental health, special education and other services to those children. In 1994, U.S. District Judge David Ezra ruled Hawaii was in violation of the law. In a consent decree settling the lawsuit, the state agreed to create an expansive system to provide those services over the next 6 years. The **Felix Consent Decree** set out benchmarks for improvement by the state.

A court-appointed monitor overseeing the process said "major impediments" prevent the state from meeting its court-ordered obligation. The monitor, Ivor Groves, noted that the state has less than 3 months to achieve "substantial implementation" of requirements under the Felix consent decree, yet it falls short in these areas:

- Skilled professionals capable of providing timely functional assessments.
- Development of appropriate plans matched to the needs of the child.
- Timely execution of plans.
- Knowledgeable professionals to appropriately address children with pervasive developmental disorders and severe behavior disorders.
- Properly structured living arrangements for children and adolescents with both developmental disability and behavior disorders.
- Distribution of resources statewide to all eligible children." (Star Bulletin, May 29, 2000, Felix decree: Problems and progress).

In May 2000, Judge Ezra found the State of Hawaii to be in contempt of court for failing to meet those obligations. One year later a 12-member bipartisan **Senate-House Felix Investigation Committee** was set up, charged with tracking the more than $1.4 billion in funds spent since 1994, to make sure that money went for those services due special education children in the public schools. In a report, released on December 2001, the committee concluded implementation of the Felix Consent Decree had been problematic.

In December 2001, Auditor Marion Higa released a report saying that the state's response to the Felix Consent Decree "has not achieved the expected results." The Auditor stated, "The system of care focused more on procedural compliance rather than on an effective system to help the children. In addition, the system is largely based on treatments that cannot demonstrate effectiveness." The report stated that the departments of Health and Education did not provide a full picture of the costs of complying with the Felix Consent Decree and lacked adequate financial management infrastructure to support the compliance effort.

4.2.2 Hawaii Mental Health

The State of Hawaii provides mental health services to children and youth through a system of care that includes both school-based services provided by the Department of Education (DOE) and an array of more intensive mental health services contracted by the Department of Health (DOH) Child and Adolescent Mental Health Division (CAMHD). The Hawaii State DOH is organized into three administrations: Behavioral Health Services, Health Resources, and Environmental Health. The CAMHD is a division of the DOH Behavioral

Health Services Administration, which also includes the Adult Mental Health Division and the Alcohol and Drug Abuse Division (http://hawaii.gov/health/mental-health/camhd/index.html).

The mission of CAMHD is to provide timely and effective mental health prevention, assessment and treatment services to children and youth with emotional and behavioral challenges, and their families. There are 17 CCCs in Hawaii (8 on Oahu, 4 on Maui, 4 on Hawaii Island, 1 on Kauai) who usually meet once a month. Parent support groups, workshops, and informational meetings on pertinent subjects are common activities locally. Conferences and special events are offered throughout the year.

Legislation in 1994 mandated that the State of Hawaii create a system of care (including special education services) for children with emotional and behavioral disorders and their families. A major outcome of this ruling—due to a "leadership-initiated response to improve service quality and efficiency" (in press, p. 3)—was to identify and implement evidence-based services in the system of care. To help accomplish this goal, the Hawaii Department of Health Child and Adolescent (CAMHD) established the CAMHD Empirical Basis to Services (EBS) Task Force. This Task Force continues to drive the evidence based services initiative, and is further summarized in Chorpita et al. (2002).

The initiative identifies empirically supported programs (such as Multisystemic Therapy) while also seeking out common components of evidence based services that can be duplicated in routine care. The initiative provides course definition and treatment selection; implements specific evidence based services; encourages the use of evidence based services; provides large scale training, performance standards and practice guidelines; and utilizes information systems, performance measures, and feedback tools. Chorpita et al. (2002) provide a summary of evidence based services identified by the Task Force, and Daleiden and Chorpita (2005) discuss strategies used by CAMHD to manage evidence based clinical decision making (See also Chorpita and Taylor 2001; Chorpita et al. 2005; Daleiden et al. 2006).

Within the CAMHD of the Hawaii Department of Health, its new Director, Tina Donkervoet brought with her a style of data- and system-minded leadership that she had been immersed in at the Medical University of South Carolina, while her husband, John, worked at the Family Services Research Center (FSCR), which was headed by Scott Henggeler, the developer of MST. It was Tina's leadership that established the Hawaii Empirical Basis to Services Task Force in 1999. This group aimed to provide an interdisciplinary evaluation of interventions for common youth disorders based on controlled treatment studies found in the scientific literature. The primary methodology, procedures, and criteria used were adapted from various related efforts, including the Task Force on Promotion and Dissemination of Psychological Procedures, Division of Clinical Psychology, American Psychological Association (1995) and the Empirically Supported Psychosocial Interventions for Children Task Force (1998).

As the national policy landscape became increasingly focused on closing the gap between research and practice across all mental health (e.g., Hogan 2003; Institute

of Medicine 2001; National Advisory Mental Health Council Workgroup on Child
and Adolescent Mental Health Intervention Development and Deployment 2001;
NAMHC Workgroup on Services Research and Clinical Epidemiology 2006) the
EBS Task Force kept abreast of this progress.

When, after reviewing the available options, the EBS Task force recommended
the adoption of MST to meet the mental health needs of Hawaiian adolescents,
CAMHD, jumped right in with RFPs for several teams. There was no pilot testing although some local officials expressed concerns about how MST would fit
within the Island culture. However it did not take very long for CAMHD to discover some weaknesses in its provider network. Eventually there were only two
private providers that provide MST:

Parents And Children Together (PACT), which was founded in 1968, is one
of Hawaii's leading non-profit organizations providing a wide array of innovative
and educational social services to families in need. Assisting more than 16,000
people annually, PACT helps families identify, address and successfully resolve
challenges through its 15 statewide programs. Among its services are treatment
programs, support for domestic abuse victims, youth activities, financial and child
literacy programs and initiatives for early childhood education. PACT offers 15
programs in the following service areas:

- Child Abuse and Neglect Prevention and Treatment
- Community Building and Economic Development
- Domestic Violence Prevention and Treatment
- Early Childhood Education
- Economic Development
- Teen Leadership Development
- Mental Health Support

The Institute for Family Enrichment, known as TIFFE, is a local organization
founded in 1981 in Honolulu, Hawaii. Twenty-eight years ago with a mission to
provide creative and effective training and services for children and families in
Hawaii. TIFFE now operates from the corporate office in Honolulu, with local
office sites in Kaneohe, Hilo, Kealakekua Kona, and Pahoa on the Big Island.
Their prevention program services are available on every island in the state while
specialized intervention and treatment programs are available on Oahu and the
Big Island, with training and education services available statewide. From its five
founders in 1981, TIFFE now has over 370 staff statewide providing an array of
services for and on behalf of children, adolescents, adults and families across the
state of Hawaii.

It took a while for the impact of the new evidence based approach to become
visible. The most rapid improvement occurred during the middle years of the
reform, in which "the measured improvement became evident after a period of
administrative reorganization and rapid capacity expansion, and during the period
of expanded care coordination, performance management and information systems
development" (Daleiden et al. 2006). The evidence based services initiative began
halfway through this period of improvement.

Quarterly outcome measures used to access child and service system character-istics included the Child and Adolescent Functional Assessment Scale (CAFAS), the Child and Adolescent Level of Care Utilization System (CALOCUS), and the parent, teacher, and youth report forms of the Achenbach System of Empirically Based Assessment (ASEBA). During the period FY 2002–2004, youth (N = 500) were admitted with average clinical impairment scores of ~110 on the CAFAS; youth were maintained at a moderate level of impairment (~85) and discharged with an average CAFAS Total score of ~60. A rate of change calculation revealed that youth were getting better. "The median rate of improvement nearly tri-pled over the four-year period, whereas the mean rate approximately doubled" (Daleiden et al. 2006).

Similar rates of improvement were found for the CALOCUS and ASEBA. From FY 2002–2005, the average length of services was reduced by 40–60 %, and the average length of service reduced most rapidly from FY 2002–2004. For example, youth went from an average length of service from 866 days in 2002 to 434 days in 2004. Average expenditures were also reduced from FY 2002–2005. Costs reduced from $1083 per point of improvement in the CAFAS during 2002 to $650 in 2005.

In summary, the Hawaii system of care has "improved dramatically" (in press, p. 13) over the past decade. "Efforts to implement evidence based services, develop care coordination practice, increase information feedback to stakeholders, adopt statewide performance measures, restructure quality improvement and prac-tice-focused performance management processes, and improve utilization manage-ment appear to be meeting with success" (Daleiden et al. 2006).

In April 2004, U.S. District Judge Ezra approved a plan to end court oversight of special education in Hawaii's public schools. Judge Ezra, stating that the state is in "substantial compliance" with federal law, agreed to reduce court oversight under the Felix Consent Decree in anticipation of dismissing the class-action case in 2005.

On May 27, 2005, the case was officially closed under a plan approved by U.S. District Judge David Ezra, freeing the Hawaii state departments of Education and Health from 12 years of court oversight.

Chapter 5
Maine and New Mexico: Small Centralized Systems are Easier to Change

5.1 Maine: Centralized and Networked

The use of Evidence-Based Practices (EBP) in Maine's juvenile justice system cannot easily be traced to any one event or act of legislation. However, the success that Maine has achieved in utilizing EBP has been greatly facilitated by the tradition of collaboration and strong leadership that exists in the state. The main motivation for the push for EBP began in the mid-1990s during a fiscal crisis in which cost-savings were needed and leadership began to recognize that the current approach was ineffective. Several major stakeholders and groups have led the way for Maine, including: the Maine Juvenile Justice Advisory Group; the Maine Department of Corrections; the Maine Juvenile Justice Task Force; the Maine Judiciary, the Maine School of Law; and the Muskie School of Public Service at the University of Southern Maine. The work of these groups has relied on substantial buy-in and support from the legislature, and cross-agency collaboration that has been found in the state for many years. These elements have gone a long way toward developing an evidence-based culture in Maine.

Maine's court system is "unified", with 32 district courts that handle juvenile cases. Juvenile justice is administered by the Maine Department of Corrections, Division of Juvenile Services. "An Associate Commissioner for Juvenile Services oversees all aspects of the Division, which include the functions of court diversion, detention, probation supervision, commitments, and aftercare services" (Hennings 2007, p. 2). The juvenile justice system is thus operated under a centralized format in Maine. There are three regional offices in Maine (Bangor, Portland, and Augusta) and two secure placement facilities in the central and southern portions of the state. Juveniles can be waived to adult court for a variety of reasons, but are limited to felonies, including homicide. The decision to waive juveniles rests solely with the judicial branch, though prosecutors can recommend waiver.

P. Greenwood, *Evidence-Based Practice in Juvenile Justice*,
SpringerBriefs in Translational Criminology, DOI: 10.1007/978-1-4614-8908-5_5,
© The Author(s) 2014

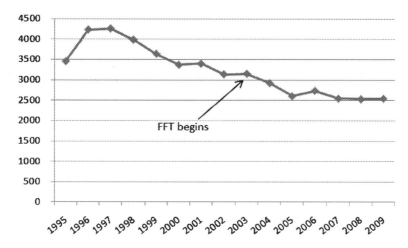

Fig. 5.1   Change in juvenile arrest rates in maine, 1995–2009. *Note* Data derived from the FBI's UCR program (criminal justice information services)

Individuals up to age 21 may stay in the juvenile justice system provided they committed their offense as a juvenile and the stipulations of the sentence call for a non-waiver. Juveniles are eligible for diversion if they commit a misdemeanor as a first time offense; in addition, juveniles may be diverted for additional offenses based upon various risk factors. Maine includes a provision for "shock incarceration" which allows confinement for 30 days. Diversion is based upon a needs assessment approach. Upon diversion, juveniles may be referred to various programs, including the volunteer-based Community Resolution Teams. Juvenile Community Corrections Officers (JCCO), perform a wide array of duties, including supervisory and assessment services to juveniles in the system and referrals to programs. There are 46 JCCOs covering the entire state (Stoodley 2012).

Maine has historically had a lower crime rate than much of the country. In 2010, the Maine UCR report showed that the total crime rate was only 26.09 per 1,000. In addition, there were 24 homicides in the entire state during that year. In 2009, Maine's crime rate of 25.34 was approximately 9 points lower than the national average of 34.85. Interestingly, however, the crime rate in Maine actually increased by 3.7 % from 2009 to 2010. In terms of juvenile crime, the most recent juvenile recidivism report tracked three cohorts of youths processed by Maine's justice system for the first time. The cohorts ranged in size from 1,480 in 2006 to 1,246 in 2008. One year recidivism (defined as "a re-adjudication (juvenile system) or conviction (adult system) for a new offense committed by a youth in Maine within 3 years after release from DJS supervision" (Noreus 2012, p. 1) rates for those youth placed under supervision were 21.1 % in 2006, 26.4 % in 2007, and 21.8 % in 2008 (Noreus 2011). Finally, according to a report by Rubin et al. (2009), juvenile arrests have declined by nearly 40 % over the last decade, following a national trend. Figure 5.1 displays the percentage change in arrests since 1995.

5.1.1 Juvenile Justice in Maine

When juveniles enter the criminal justice system, they are assessed using evidence-based risk assessment instruments, such as the Youth Level of Service/Case Management Inventory and—in the two youth detention centers—the Massachusetts Youth Screening Instrument (MAYSI). Leadership is working to implement the MAYSI in juvenile community corrections in the future. These instruments are used to place the juvenile under the appropriate model of care (National Center for Juvenile Justice 2005), which is usually guided by the individual's JCCO.

Maine's transformation in juvenile justice to a focus on EBP and prevention was the result of several influential actors and an increasing recognition that the current approach was not sustainable. In the early 1990s, several factors coalesced, resulting in a culture-change of sorts. After a period of increased costs due to rising numbers of inmates, which led to additional prisons being built, as well as a fiscal crisis, a new direction was needed (Rooks 1996). A watershed moment occurred with the hiring of Joseph Lehman as the Commissioner of Corrections in the 1996 and his appointment of Mary Ann Saar as Associate Commissioner of Juvenile Corrections. These actors early on began to push for evidence-based programming in juvenile corrections and a larger role for research. Lehman, in particular, at a time when few shared his view, argued that prevention programs could be far more cost-efficient than secure confinement (Rooks 1996).

One of the primary leaders in the push for EBP in Maine's Juvenile Correctional System has been Bartlett Stoodley. As a district supervisor he and other stakeholders within the Maine Department of Corrections (MDOC) were exposed to the work of Don Andrews and Ed Latessa and their notion of the "principles of effective intervention". According to Stoodley "this was like a light going on" (Stoodley 2012). In 1998, Stoodley gained permission to pilot one of the first evidence-based instruments used in the state, the Youth Level of Service Inventory. He drew on the technical support of academics at the University of Cincinnati and was able to gather widespread support throughout child-based agencies in Maine. The use of Blueprints programs was facilitated at this time by increased knowledge gained from an EBP training in Colorado, attended by MDOC leadership. In addition, juvenile recidivism studies were initiated in the late 1990s, prompting MDOC leadership to explore programs that could reduce recidivism. With ever-shrinking budgets, it became even more important to focus funds on programs that were proven to work (Stoodley 2012). Stoodley was able to continue his push for EBP when he was appointed as Associate Commissioner of Juvenile Corrections in 2000, a position he currently holds.

In terms of influential policy or acts of legislation, two stand out. First, in 1995, the MDOC made a decision to separate the juvenile from the adult system. This move allowed a more direct focus on youth specific issues and the needs of individuals who have not yet led a life of crime. In addition, the national Juvenile Justice and Delinquency Prevention Act of 2002 has also been key for Maine's work in EBP. This Act recognized the importance of early intervention and evidence based programs. It provides funds for states to carry out implementation and evaluation projects.

The Maine Department of Corrections, Division of Juvenile Services is the state agency that provides EBP services. There is a dedicated Quality Improvement team that focuses on fidelity to models. In terms of programs advocated by the 'Blueprints for Violence Prevention' report (hereafter Blueprints programs), Maine utilizes Multidimensional Treatment Foster Care (MTFC), which is offered by one service provider; Multisystemic Treatment (MST), offered by three service providers; Functional Family Therapy (FFT), offered by two service providers across the state; and Aggression Replacement Therapy (ART), which is provided in Maine's two juvenile correctional facilities and two additional agencies offering child services (King 2012; Rubin 2012).

The first Blueprint program to be adopted in Maine was MST in 1999 under one agency. Commissioner Stoodley made flexible funds available for start-up costs to cover training, clinician's time and early recruitment. Unfortunately, after completion of initial training and recruitment this early program was not operated with fidelity and was thus discontinued until other agencies were willing to take up the work (Stoodley 2012). FFT began in 2003 as a result of the efforts of an agency which proposed to use it for the most high risk juveniles. According to Stoodley, this represented a terrific opportunity that the MDOC wanted to use to their advantage. FFT "flourished" and began to achieve excellent results very quickly. EBPs such as FFT have been able to continue thanks to the willingness of other agencies to make referrals outside of MDOC. The use of MTFC was initiated in Maine in 2006 and continues to this day. Another evidence based initiative, the Problematic Sexual Behavior program, was initiated in the early 2000s in part as the result of collaboration with Sue Righthand, an associate professor at the University of Maine, Orono and research consultant who was interested in implementing it for sex offenders in Maine. The MDOC tracks outcomes such as the number of youth served by particular programs, the number of youth who have completed programs and the recidivism rate of each program. For the most part, Blueprints programs have resulted in lower recidivism rates than other similar youths who are not in such programs (Stoodley 2012).

In terms of evidence-based research, leadership within the Maine DOC has also been involved in a national initiative to standardize definitions of recidivism. This initiative is intended to facilitate comparisons of juvenile justice programs across states. The results of this work were published as a White Paper by the Council of Juvenile Correctional Administrators (Harris et al. 2009). Finally, in recent years, the philosophy of juvenile corrections in Maine has shifted. According to new commissioner Joseph Ponte, "If you look at the change in juvenile corrections, we went from a custody operation to a treatment operation" (Tapley 2011).

Similar to other states that are leading the nation in the use and evaluation of evidence-based programs, Maine has a strong history of collaboration between independent researchers and state government agencies (King 2012). For example, the Maine DOC has worked closely with professionals and researchers across diverse agencies and organizations in Maine, taking advantage of expertise where available. In particular (as noted above), the DOC has worked with the University of Maine, Orono and the Muskie School of Public Service at the University of Southern Maine for over a decade. These partnerships have allowed Maine not only to develop the organizational capacity to implement programs but also to evaluate them neutrally. According to Stoodley (2012), the use and continuation of EBP in MDOC "never would have worked were it not for the DOC making funds available for startup costs and for the willing participation of our collaborators". These collaborators have been instrumental in providing services as well as research support. It is to the research partnerships that we now turn.

5.1.2 The University of Maine, Orono

Maine is particularly advanced with respect to programs aimed at juveniles at risk for or charged with committed sex offenses. Much of this work has been the result of collaboration with the University of Maine, Orono, particularly with the department of psychology. Around the time that the Maine DOC was beginning to push for EBP within the juvenile correctional system, the state contracted with Sue Righthand and the University of Maine, Orono to conduct a literature review (Righthand and Welch 2001), a needs assessment, and offer recommendations for evidence-based programs related to juvenile sex offenders, as well as an assessment of current programming in the state (Righthand et al. 2001). This work led to the development of the Sexual Behavior Treatment Program, which was implemented at Maine's two correctional centers, and also opened up opportunities for additional consultations and trainings, paving the way for a later grant (described above). The grant provided funds and assistance for state-wide correctional practitioners and other professionals to be trained in the Juvenile Sex Offender Assessment Protocol (J-SOAP) (Prentky and Righthand 2003), a version of which (J-SOAP-II) has been validated in subsequent research (Viljoen et al. 2012). In addition, the MDOC collaborated with the University of Maine, Orono with respect to a 2007 grant to assess the needs of the state for juvenile sex offending programming and to offer recommendations. This work recommended and provided assistance for additional ART, MST, and CPAI training.

Pre-post assessments have shown that these efforts have reduced risk factors. In addition, evaluations of the Sexual Behavior Treatment Program using the CPAI have resulted in very satisfactory ratings (indicating a high degree of adherence to evidence-based principles). Maine is researching the use of Trauma Focused CBT in juvenile corrections populations, which is an evidence-based program directed toward youth who have experienced abuse (Righthand 2012). The Maine DOC, in conjunction with the University of Maine, is researching the use of Trauma Affect Regulation Guide for Education and Treatment (TARGET) in juvenile corrections populations (Righthand 2012). The state has previously experimented with the TARGET in select juvenile correctional populations. TARGET is a program that has not yet achieved evidence-based status but research shows it may have the potential to become an EBP in the future (SAMHSA 2007).

5.1.3 Muskie School of Public Service, University of Southern Maine

Prior to 2009, the Muskie School of Public Service's research projects were located among three distinct research institutes that operated largely in silos. These were merged into one institute 3 years ago in order to facilitate partnerships and sharing of resources (Dorsey 2012a). In total, the institute employs roughly 200 individuals and is conducts local and national research in numerous areas, including public health, disability and aging, children youth and families and justice (Nalli et al. 2011).

The Muskie School has been an integral research partner during the development of EBP in Maine's juvenile corrections system. Muskie School staff has experience with criminal justice research and evaluation projects on a national and state level. One of the central contributions of the Muskie School is the quantitative justice research conducted by the Maine Statistical Analysis Center (SAC) which is housed at the university and is an objective, independent "research, evaluation and analysis service that identifies and tracks selected criminal justice trends in Maine" (Dorsey 2012b, p. 1). In addition, the staff has expertise in numerous areas including public policy and management, planning, social work, public health, law, sociology, and anthropology. Muskie staff is trained in implementing the Correctional Program Assessment Inventory (CPAI), which is based upon the principles of effective intervention (Matthews et al. 2001). The Muskie School was also able, as a result of funds available from a grant, to train additional professionals across the state in 2009 to conduct CPAIs.

5.1.3.1 Collaboration with the MDOC

A key development in the partnership between the Muskie School and the DOC occurred in 2003. Prior to that point in time, data tracking systems used by the DOC were not adequate for proper research. The Maine DOC, with the help of the Muskie School, developed the Corrections Information System (CORIS), which is a state of the art web-based offender management system that may be tapped for research and evaluation. CORIS includes data on over 60,000 individuals under supervision of the Maine correctional system. The system allows standardized access to these data, which facilitates research and evaluation of correctional programs. The database generates necessary data used to facilitate research projects, including the juvenile recidivism and disproportionate minority contact report series.

The approach the Maine DOC and the Muskie School take to EBP is drawn from the best practice literature and the principles of effective intervention. Close attention is paid to contextual factors such as organizational capacity, staff availability and needs, in order to ensure that programs are implemented in such a way that they have the best chance of succeeding. Programs are selected on the basis of thorough research on what other states and similar locales are currently doing and from the research base. Once programs are in place, the Muskie School is able to offer independent and unbiased evaluations which result in recommendations for improvement and information that may be shared with other states. Muskie School staff and partners have been integral in the use of CPAIs to assess how well Maine's juvenile justice programs are adhering to the principles of effective intervention.

Because of the goal of research neutrality and transparency, research conducted using DOC data is made available to a broad array of stakeholders and to the general public. In addition, the Muskie School disseminates their reports to the Maine legislature, which can then translate their findings into effective legislation.

5.1.4 National Institute of Corrections Project

The Maine DOC received a technical assistance award from the National Institute of Corrections and was made a site for a pilot project along with one other state in 2003. While this project focused on adult corrections, it was crucial to the work of the DOC overall and served to highlight work that is ongoing in Maine with respect to EBP. To illustrate, the technical assistance award allowed the Maine DOC to organize a meeting of justice stakeholders to discuss the process of EBP adoption and the steps necessary to reduce recidivism. This was a state-and system-wide approach. The project was designed to demonstrate the then novel NIC approach of integrating EBP with organizational development and collaboration. In 2011, the Justice Policy Center released a report evaluating the project. The study used a mix of qualitative and quantitative methods, seeking to describe the changes that took place as a result of the integrated project. Information about how EBP is being implemented across the state as well as key information on how to improve processes resulted from the project.

5.1.5 Juvenile Justice Advisory Group

An important contributing factor to the development of EBP in Maine is the work of the Juvenile Justice Advisory Group (JJAG). The JJAG has been a powerful voice advocating best practices, evaluation and dissemination of data to ensure juveniles are provided the most effective treatments available. The JJAG is comprised of community members, corrections professionals, and community leaders, all appointed by the governor. The directives of the group are:

- To promote effective, system level responses that further the goals of the Juvenile Justice Delinquency Act;
- To promote the development of gender specific services for Maine's juvenile justice system;
- To ensure that youth are not detained for lack of appropriate alternatives;
- To reduce delinquency and youth violence by providing community members with skills, knowledge, and opportunities to foster a healthy and nurturing environment that supports the growth and development of productive and responsible citizens;
- To provide information and training to legislators, juvenile justice professionals, and the general public to benefit youth and all those involved with Maine's juvenile justice system; and
- To maintain compliance with the core requirements of the JJDP Act and to monitor the compliance of JJAG grantees (Maine Department of Juvenile Services 2006).

The JJAG includes 27 members, all of whom operate in a voluntary capacity. The mission of the JJAG is "to advise and make recommendations to state policy makers and to promote effective system level responses that further the goals of the Juvenile Justice and Delinquency Prevention Act". The JJAG is involved in several initiatives on the federal level, including the Coalition on Juvenile Justice and the Federal Advisory Committee on Juvenile Justice.

Funds administered through the JJAG were used for a variety of projects, including $95,350 for the Broadreach Family and Community Services, $75,000 for the Youthlinks; Five Town Communities that Care, $150,000 for the Riverview Foundation, the Leadership and Resiliency Project and the Youth Horizons Program, The R.E.A.L. School and Teen Aspirations Program—$105,000 (Title II, Formula Grant), and the LE^{2}AD (Lisbon Education and Delinquency Prevention) Program (Juvenile Justice Advisory Group 2010).

According to a 2010 report by the JJAG, the programs the group funds reported favorable results with regard to changes in youth behavior and attitudes. For example, the report found that 80 % of youth have shown improved school attendance, 70 % have shown improvements in substance use, and 75 % of the youth studied improved antisocial behavior (Juvenile Justice Advisory Group 2010).

5.1.6 Juvenile Justice Task Force

In 2009, the Juvenile Justice Task Force (JJTF) was formed in Maine. The chairs were the Chief Justice of the Maine Supreme Judicial Court, the First Lady, and the Dean of the Maine Law School. The originating charter, written by the Chief Justice, outlined the goals of the JJTF, which included: improving education, incarceration/detention services and access to community programs. The JJTF is currently comprised of over 70 individuals, representing diverse agencies, services, and public constituencies. In addition, staff from the Muskie School of Public Service works with the JJTF to evaluate programs and make recommendations.

According to the JJTF 2010 report, the main thrust of their work involves improving services. "Each subcommittee worked to evaluate current system practices and identify inefficiencies and gaps in services, in consideration of youth outcomes and by comparisons with nationwide best practices, before devising recommendations designed to improve juvenile service-provision and system organization in Maine" (Juvenile Justice Task Force 2010, p. 3). Thus, the JJTF is interested in improvements across a number of systems that affect juveniles.

Importantly, the JJTF recognizes the importance of early intervention and prevention strategies, not only to reduce the emergence of delinquency but also a host of negative behaviors/outcomes. This group has done a tremendous amount of work researching best practices and the benefits of particular programs or strategies. They recommend not only implementing EBP but also continuous monitoring of these programs to ensure they are as useful as possible:

> An effective quality assurance system will be efficient and non-burdensome in order to guard against inefficiency and ineffectiveness. Evaluations and reform must be conducted with an eye toward building the robust system of community-based services that Maine's at-risk and system-involved youth desperately need (Juvenile Justice Task Force 2010, p. 22).

The University of Maine School of Law is also involved with the JJTF. Christopher Northrop, JD, a faculty member of the School of Law, is the chair of the Juvenile Justice Implementation Council (JJIC). The JJIC guides program implementation of reform initiatives and programs in Maine's juvenile justice system. This council was a product of the initial work of the JJTF and is integral to the EBP work that occurs within the state.

5.1.7 Barriers and Issues in Maine

As is the case in other rural, sparsely populated states, Maine faces several unique challenges to establishing a culture of EBP in juvenile justice. One area of concern is with respect to standardization of practices and processes across the state. It is unclear whether, for example, JCCOs operate in the same way in Portland as in Presque Isle (nearly 300 miles apart). The DOC has focused on assessing this issue and promoting standardization across the system.

Perhaps the most significant issue concerns funding for EBP. The MDOC is a small agency with limited resources. This forces it to be "opportunistic" (Stoodley 2012) with respect to finding willing partners and funders for particular programs. As most states have experienced in the last few years, the state of Maine's economy has been in turmoil, with funds being cut for a variety of programs. Often, the first programs that lose funding are those that are seen as less than necessary—and sometimes EBP fall into this category. As a result of this impediment, the JJTF has developed a subcommittee whose task is specifically focused on identifying, streamlining and utilizing funds to maximize the limited monies available in Maine.

As a rural state, Maine faces other challenges such as long travel distances for clinicians and practitioners who must make home visits. EBP is hard work in ideal conditions and this is exacerbated in sparsely populated areas with few support services.

5.1.8 Lessons Learned

The state of Maine's experience with evidence-based practice illustrates that there is no one approach that fits every state. The increasing use of EBP cannot easily be traced to one specific piece of legislation or one event. Rather, it appears that a confluence of factors coalesced in the 1990s to help pave the way for an EBP culture in Maine's juvenile justice system. In particular, key leaders in the MDOC and related agencies pushed for the state to begin to use programs that had been proven effective in other locales. These and other leaders who have continued to advocate for EBP in Maine include Joseph Lehman, Mary Ann Saar, Bartlett Stoodley, and Rod Bouffard (Superintendent at Long Creek Youth Correctional Facility). In addition, the working partnership between the Maine DOC and researchers at the University of Maine, Orono and Augusta, and the Muskie School of Public Service has helped inform practitioners regarding the importance of good data systems and the process required to implement and evaluate EBP in juvenile justice.

Other factors that exist in Maine are likely to be vital for the success of an EBP culture in any state. These include a strong tradition of collaboration among private, public, and state agencies. The groups that operate many of the Blueprints programs are private organizations and have been open to outside evaluation, namely, in terms of the CPAI. In addition, having a "research arm" that contributes independent evaluation, research expertise, and assists in disseminating results to the legislature, the public and private sphere is important. In Maine, numerous state university system partners have worked together to help fulfill this role (University of Maine—Orono, University of Maine—Augusta) in addition to the University of Southern Maine's Muskie School of Public Service.

Motivation and buy-in on the part of staff is essential. In Maine, all JCCOs are trained in risk assessment and EBP and also in Motivational Interviewing. These skills are necessary to be able to gain cooperation of families who must allow seemingly "intrusive" services into their homes. Having staff who truly believe in the work helps protect the programs from withering. Finally, having diversified, adequate sources of funding remains a priority, and one that is constantly in need of attention. These are issues that each state must grapple with in order to maximize the efficiency of juvenile justice services and programs and ultimately, reduce the occurrence of crime among our youth.

5.2 New Mexico

5.2.1 Juvenile Justice in New Mexico

Juvenile justice and human services in New Mexico are all run at the state level. Juvenile Probation Officers (JPOs), employed by Children, Youth and Families Department (CYFD), work out of 29 local offices. They supervise only juveniles. The court sets the terms of probation with recommendations from the JPO, District Attorney, and the youth's attorney. JPOs maintain contact with clients in placement through phone calls, letters, and staffing the progress of treatment.

Probation is a court-order through which a juvenile is placed under the control, supervision and care of a probation field staff member in lieu of facility commitment, so long as the probationer meets certain standards of conduct. Aftercare (formerly parole) refers to the term of supervision that occurs once a juvenile is conditionally released to the community after serving a facility commitment term. Clients in aftercare are subject to being returned to detention or facility placement for rule violations or other offenses.

The philosophy driving probation practice in the state is claimed to be (CYFD website) a balanced approach with increased emphasis on treatment and front-end services rather than commitment to facilities. JPOs are not stationed in neighborhood or school-based offices. However, almost every county has a JPO office, and many JPOs have an office they use in the schools. Most offices have community support officers and JPOs who work non-traditional hours. New Mexico provides specialized probation services, including intensive supervision, with state funding. No standard sets caseload size. CYFD uses a structured decision making tool that recommends levels of probation supervision in all counties. In addition, Plan of Care Tracking is used. Juvenile Community Corrections and the Juvenile Justice Advisory Committee evaluate the effectiveness of probation programs. The legislature funds these evaluations with community corrections funding. District Courts, which are general jurisdiction courts exercise jurisdiction over delinquency proceedings. There are 13 district courts, 11 of which are multi-county. For more information, visit the http://www.nmcourts.gov.

According to Ken Warner, who was the Bureau Chief for Behavioral Health in New Mexico's Children, Youth and Families Department (CYFD) at the time, interest in EBPs in NM was stimulated by a presentation by an MST representative in 1999 or 2000. At that time the state held in residential custody many youth who CYFD leaders believed did not need to be there. MST sounded like a viable alternative. According to Ken, Larry White, a psychologist for one of the 3 Managed Care Organizations (MCOs) that served the state became a champion.

Even after a general agreement was reached among policy makers, to proceed with some MST pilots, it still took 2 years to work out the details. The two pilot sites, one in Albuquerque, the other in Santa Fe, were run by different providers. The MCOs handled the referrals. Initial training was covered by OJJDP block grant funds. Providers were initially paid on a fee for service basis.

As the two pilot sites began to produce favorable outcomes other MST teams were established throughout the state. By 2008 they had 4–6 providers, each with 2 teams. Unlike other large rural states such as Arizona, NM has been able to support teams in many of its smaller communities. Some of these teams may be only 2 therapists and a supervisor. Ken feels that the critical factor in spreading MST was in getting the state Medicaid Plan amended to provide an explicit rate for MST. At one point NM probation and parole decided to try and run several FFT programs in-house. For unknown reasons the effort was discontinued. Since the initial launch of MST there has been a succession of 3 managed care providers, with Optum Health holding the current contract. Value Options preceded them.

In July 2001, New Mexico's Medicaid Behavioral Health system implemented a program to provide funding for Multisystemic Therapy (MST) treatment for New Mexico's mental health and Juvenile Justice involved youth. New Mexico's Children, Youth and Families Department (CYFD) also provided funding for the development and implementation of the program evaluation component for MST teams in New Mexico. According to David Bernstein, who directs the Center for Effective Intervention (CEI), Keller Strother, MST Services CEO, was directly involved in the initial launch of MST in N.M., with Marshall doing the initial site assessment. State officials and the managed care provider decided where the first programs would be located (Santa Fe and Albuquerque and picked the providers.

When it became clear that MST would be expanding in NM, MST brought in CEI, one of the initial MST network partners, to handle the training and TA. Network Partners are organizations with a strong record of starting and implementing MST programs that collaborate with MST Services to meet the growing demand for MST training. These locally controlled groups are committed to making sure that the MST treatment model is followed with integrity and without variation so that the best outcomes can be realized. They also play an important role in shaping research on treatment effectiveness, transportability and dissemination. MST Network Partner organizations employ staffs that are fully trained in program development. MST Services maintains an ongoing working relationship with each partner that focuses on staff development, quality improvement and quality assurance. David says his initial contract for training and oversight was with the BH contractor under block grant funding. He now contracts directly with local agencies.

The Center for Effective Interventions (CEI) was created in December 2000 and is part of the Human Services Department at Metropolitan State College of Denver. CEI works with communities and agencies providing technical assistance leading to the selection of models of practice to create or enhance a continuum of research-based practices.

Beginning with a mission to disseminate Multisystemic Therapy (MST) throughout Colorado, the office has grown to provide support and training to MST teams in New Mexico, Texas, Arizona, and Oklahoma. In addition, CEI is in the process of developing relationships with other evidence-based and promising program models. To date they have developed working agreements with Functional Family Therapy and Multidimensional Treatment Foster Care.

5.2.1.1 The New Mexico Behavioral Health Collaborative

The Collaborative was created by Governor Bill Richardson and the New Mexico State Legislature during the 2004 Legislative Session (State Statute). The Legislation allows several state agencies and resources involved in behavioral health prevention, treatment and recovery to work as one in an effort to improve mental health and substance abuse services in New Mexico. This cabinet-level group represents 15 state agencies and the Governor's office.

The vision of the Collaborative is to be a single statewide behavioral health delivery system in which funds are managed effectively and efficiently and to create an environment in which the support of recovery and development of resiliency is expected, mental health is promoted, the adverse affects of substance abuse and mental illness are prevented or reduced, and behavioral health consumers are assisted in participating fully in the lives of their communities. Linda Roebuck, the Collaborative's CEO, is responsible for turning vision into reality in the lives of New Mexican families.

The Collaborative is charged with a number of responsibilities including:

* Inventorying all expenditures for mental health and substance abuse services;
* Creating a single behavioral health care and services delivery system that promotes mental health, emphasizes prevention, early intervention, resiliency, recovery and rehabilitation and funds are managed efficiently, and ensures availability of services throughout the State;
* Paying special attention to regional, cultural, rural, frontier, urban and border issues, and seeking and considering suggestions of Native Americans;
* Contracting with a single, Statewide services purchasing entity (SE); Monitoring service capacities and utilization in order to achieve desired performance measures and outcomes;
* Making decisions regarding funds, interdepartmental staff, grant writing and grants management;
* Comprehensive planning and meeting State and federal requirements;
* Overseeing systems of care, data management, performance and outcome indicators, rate setting, services definitions, considering consumer, family and citizen input, monitoring training, assuring that evidence-based practices receive priority, and providing oversight for fraud and abuse and licensing and certification.

5.2.2 The New Mexico MST Outcomes Tracking Project July 2005 -December 2010

Implementation began in late 2003. In March 2005, the New Mexico Outcomes Tracking Project (NM-OTP) combined efforts and resources with Colorado's Center for Effective Interventions (CEI), which had contracted with Focus Research and Evaluation to create and pilot a statewide outcomes database for youth who received MST treatment in Colorado. The MST Institute (MSTI) joined the collaboration early in the development phase. The collaboration ultimately produced the Colorado/New Mexico (CO/NM) Enhanced MSTI Website. This site, which is available through the national MSTI website, allows clinicians easy access to data entry and routine reporting, and complies with appropriate rules and regulations that protect families' and agencies' privacy and confidentiality. The New Mexico MST Outcomes Tracking Project documents demographic and outcome data regarding youth and families who have received MST services from ten provider agencies.

Partners involved in the New Mexico MST Outcomes Tracking Project (NM-MST-OTP) were:

- New Mexico's Children, Youth and Families Department (CYFD)—provides co-leadership, coordination and funding for the program evaluation.
- The Center for Effective Interventions (CEI) –provides support, training, and consultation to MST teams in New Mexico and surrounding western states. CEI shares leadership and funding of the program evaluation.
- Focus Research and Evaluation—an independent program evaluation consulting practice based in Colorado.
- MST Institute (MSTI)—a non-profit organization that provides web-based information and quality assurance tools to programs implementing MST.

Also participating are eleven New Mexico MST provider agencies with 20 teams:

- Border Area Mental Health Services (BAMHS), Silver City (one team)
- Carlsbad Mental Health Center, Carlsbad (one team)
- Counseling Associates, Inc., Roswell (one team)
- Families and Youth, Inc. (FYI), Las Cruces (one team)
- Guidance Center of Lea County, Hobbs (one team)
- Mcsilla Valley Outpatient (MVO), Las Cruces and surrounding communities (two teams)
- Southwest Family Guidance Center and Institute, Albuquerque (two teams)
- TeamBuilders, Clovis/Portales (two teams), Las Vegas (one team), greater Santa Fe/Española (one team)
- The Santa Fe Community Guidance Center –Santa Fe and northeastern New Mexico (five teams)
- University of New Mexico (UNM), Albuquerque (two teams).

Note: Providers and teams change over time. This list includes the MST Providers and the number of teams represented by each in the database used for this report.

5.2.3 Outcomes

The results of this 5 and one-half year evaluation were very positive. Although the youth demonstrated very high rates of severity at admission across multiple life domains, a set of repeated measures analyses conducted for youth who completed

MST and for whom there was data at admission, discharge, and 6 and 12 months after discharge, showed statistically significant improvement from admission to discharge in all areas studied, including Arrests, Overall Legal and Mental Health and Substance Abuse problems, as well as in instrumental indicators of youth and family functioning. These gains were maintained for at least 12 months after youth were discharged from MST. Further analyses also demonstrated reduced utilization of and costs averted associated with two common out of home placements as well as a likelihood of not recidivating (i.e., receipt of a petition) of 95 % 1 year after completing MST treatment. These findings demonstrate noteworthy successes across 23 counties representing New Mexico's geographic, ethnic, and economic diversity, and are consistent with other positive findings of outcomes of MST treatment with juvenile justice involved youth.

5.2.4 Other Program Models

FFT has not been successful in NM. Most of the programs that started up closed because they were not getting paid enough. David thinks it would be hard to build a second network (for FFT) in such a small state. He holds a steering committee meeting every 2 months for all the MST providers along the Optum Health and state officials. Claims it is very useful in working problems.

Although NM has done very well with MST, they have not picked up NFP or MTFC, preferring to use local home visitation and a therapeutic foster care program that costs even more than MTFC. They also use a lot of Wraparound Milwaukee (WM). Wraparound Milwaukee is a service delivery program that integrates the mental health, juvenile justice, and other systems to address the mental health needs of juvenile justice system clientele (average age 14–15) and parental problems at the same time. WM began by providing services to youth and their families in the mental health system. Now it is a county-operated collaborative that provides comprehensive care to youth referred from both the child welfare and juvenile justice systems and their families. Wraparound Milwaukee serves as the hub of a comprehensive system linking several human service agencies, thus forming a managed-care continuum of treatment options. The program currently serves more than 650 youth, 400 of whom are adjudicated delinquent. The program model is endorsed by: The Center for Effective Collaboration and Practice, American Institutes for Research and the National Gang Center and the OJJDP Model Programs Guide as a Promising Program, but it is not listed by Blueprints (not even on their program Matrix) or DOJ's Crime Solutions.

The use of blended funding has been particularly important to the success of the Wraparound Milwaukee program. The project is sustained by pooled funds that come from the system partners in this integrated, multi-service approach to meeting the needs of youths and their families. The fact that the involved agencies share the expenses of the program helps enormously to break down barriers to system integration. The program receives a flat monthly fee for each client and must pay for all treatment services, including incarceration and residential care. In 1999, the program received more than $26 million in pooled funds. After all funds are pooled and "de-categorized", the program can use them to cover any services that families need, in a mix of formal and informal services. This approach helps ensure that the most appropriate services are purchased and gives project staff an incentive to keep as many youth as possible in their homes. The program has shown delinquency reductions among clients in a before-after study.

5.2.5 *Juvenile Justice Program Inventory*

The New Mexico Criminal and Juvenile Justice Coordinating Council developed the New Mexico Sentencing Commission, http://nmsc.unm.edu/ an online searchable database of programs for juveniles referred to the New Mexico Children, Youth and Families Departments (CYFD) Juvenile Justice Services. Users can obtain basic information about each program includingt: program name, contact information, description, eligibility, ages served, capacity, funding sources, CYFD contract division (if contracted through CYFD), non-profit status, CYFD client populations, areas of the state served, and types of services offered.

5.2.5.1 Delinquency Intake Screening

Juvenile Probation Officers from the New Mexico Children, Youth and Families Department, Youth and Family Services receive and examine law enforcement delinquency complaints and conduct preliminary inquiries (PI) to determine how to proceed. The PI determines the best interests of the youth and the public regarding any action taken. Intake must notify the District Attorney of all felony complaints along with any recommended adjustments to the complaint. The county District Attorney, after consulting with probation, must endorse the filing and subsequently sign all petitions.

5.2.5.2 Diversion

By statute (32A-2-7), during the preliminary inquiry on a delinquency complaint, Juvenile Probation Officers from the New Mexico Children, Youth and Families Department, Youth and Family Services may refer youth to an appropriate agency, and adjustment conferences may be held instead of filing petitions. At the beginning of the preliminary inquiry, the parties must be advised of their basic statutory rights, and no party may be compelled to appear at any conference, produce any papers, or visit any place. If the juvenile completes the agreed upon conditions and no new charges are filed against the juvenile, the pending petition is dismissed.

Juvenile Probation Officers have the power to informally dispose of up to three misdemeanor charges brought against a youth within 2 years.

5.2.5.3 Predisposition Investigation/Client Family Baseline Interviews

Juvenile Probation Officers from the New Mexico Children, Youth and Families Department, Youth and Family Services prepare predisposition reports for the court to consider at disposition. New Mexico uses a structured decision making formula when making disposition recommendations and determining appropriate levels of supervision to provide uniformity statewide for handling cases. The state focuses on three areas of rehabilitation: education, cognitive restructuring, and mental health care. For more information, visit the Children's Research Center of the National Council on Crime and Delinquency.

5.2.5.4 Direct Placement

In New Mexico, the court can place a juvenile directly in a Residential Treatment Center (RTC), group home, or other type of treatment setting without committing the juvenile to Children, Youth and Families. Such commitment is for the duration of treatment. The court and the Juvenile Probation Officer (JPO) make the release decision. The JPO in charge of the youth's probation supervises the juvenile while in direct placement.

The decade old Santa Fe Regional Juvenile Justice Board (SFRJJB) is served by community members from diverse backgrounds, who are appointed by the Mayor and City Council. Program planning, service integration, data analysis and program evaluations are the primary functions of the Board to address youth issues in a comprehensive and coordinated manner. The Board is one of twelve "Continuum Sites" from around the state and is funded by the New Mexico Children, Youth and Families Department (CYFD). The Continuum Sites provide their respective communities with Alternatives to Detention Initiatives and/or Youth At-Risk services.

Chapter 6
Louisiana: A Model for Change

Louisiana's story may be the most dramatic of all our lead states. The total system overhaul and reform, although long overdue, became much more urgent under pressure from a lawsuit against the state brought by the Federal Department of Justice. DOJ's investigation of the state's juvenile detention facilities revealed a severe lack of appropriate medical and mental health services. It was similar to the crisis regarding "conditions of care" in Connecticut but with the added pressure of a federal lawsuit.

In a multi-faceted approach combining both state and local partnerships, as well as outside support, Louisiana has, for the most part, successfully addressed the complexities of aligning multiple systems and stakeholders. They have built a more collaborative process similar to that described as critical by Chamberlain et al. (2011) and Fixen (2009). As in other top states, Louisiana also has a strong intermediary academic institution, Louisiana State University, working in collaboration with local practitioners. What makes them distinctly unique is the rapid speed with which they emerged from the depths of the traditional correctional model to overwhelming statewide support for evidence-based practices and whole-child, custodial care, resulting in a cohesive effort of all stakeholders towards changing what doesn't work and replacing it with what does.

In summary, Louisiana appears to be an authentic model of reform success, combining both state and local partnerships in a cohesive use of their resources, while utilizing EPB's and best-practice approaches. Circumstance and timing aligned with the support of people in key leadership and political roles, creating the perfect opportunity to bring statewide awareness to evidence-based practices and creating an indisputable, data-driven "how-to" EBP template for others to follow.

6.1 Introduction

Louisiana is the 31st most extensive and 25th most populous of the 50 United States. Its capital is Baton Rouge and largest city is New Orleans. It is the only state in the US with political subdivisions termed parishes, which are local governments

P. Greenwood, *Evidence-Based Practice in Juvenile Justice*,
SpringerBriefs in Translational Criminology, DOI: 10.1007/978-1-4614-8908-5_6,
© The Author(s) 2014

equivalent to counties. In total gross state product in 2010 Louisiana was ranked 24th in the nation. It's per capita personal income, $30,952, ranked 41st.

Prior to major juvenile justice system reforms in the late 1990s, Louisiana's juvenile justice system was modeled on its adult system, which was a correctional, custodial model. It relied heavily on residential and institutional care for youth involved with the juvenile justice system. During the 1990s, Louisiana had the highest rate of incarceration per capita for juveniles with 582 per 100,000 youth in a juvenile correctional facility (Trupin 2006). This number of incarcerated youth included the placement of moderate and low level offenders in addition to those whose primary problems were exacerbated and/or caused by mental illness or substance abuse. In other words, there were scores of youth who needed other forms of care and were not receiving it.

There were also youths who didn't belong in secure care or in the system at all, but for whom no other alternatives were available, either at local or state level. Until landmark legislative changes lead to dramatic reforms by mandating immediate change, mental health and substance abuse services available to youth and their families, in their communities were severely lacking. This left very little in terms of support for at-risk children and families in need, while services for youths incarcerated in residential facilities and secure care, were all but non-existent. "It was horrible what was happening to those kids," explains DePrato, who was the first to bring EBPs to Louisiana. The state had gotten by for a long time, with services that were virtually non-existent, at both the community and state facility level. The lawsuit alleged that the state failed to provide reasonably safe conditions and adequate educational, medical, dental, mental health, and rehabilitative services It had become a matter of civil rights for incarcerated youths.

Because of the perceived need for rapid and extensive reform, caused by the lawsuit, changes began occurring rapidly as the move toward community-based alternatives was no longer an option but a requirement of the most urgent, nature. The federal lawsuit began an era of major reform initiatives in Louisiana giving voice and recognition to the quietly emerging EBP movement. As a result of the state's reform efforts, the juvenile corrections system has now downsized from over 2,000 incarcerated youth to a current population below 500. Many more youths involved with the juvenile justice system, now remain in their communities, as an alternative to incarceration, requiring stronger community-based programming.

6.2 How Reform Got Started

For years Louisiana had stood as a model for the worst-case scenario in juvenile justice policy, with an incarceration rate four times higher than the national average. With their traditional and seemingly immutable reliance on institutional care, amplified by the extreme conditions and sheer numbers of incarcerated youths, rapid reform appeared impossible. Ironically, what seemed an insurmountable wall became a well-placed, strategic stepping stone, as these intolerable conditions are what finally led to the dramatic turn of events, and eventually to Louisiana standing as a new model of reform success at its best.

The funding and technical support from the MacArthur Foundation's Models for Change Initiative, which began in 2006, was a key ingredient to this successful reform effort, but it was just as much the groundwork laid in the 10 years leading up to 2006 which enabled such compelling and rapid results, and provided a foundation for sustainable, statewide EBP growth.

The federal lawsuit, which was filed in 1997, led to a settlement agreement involving the federal DOJ, private plaintiffs, and the state. The federal judge overseeing the lawsuit in 1998, Nancy Konrad, acting on the need for immediate change, for reasons brought forth in the case, asked the Louisiana State University School of Public Health to assume responsibility for all medical, dental, mental health and rehabilitative services in the state's secure juvenile facilities. Judge Konrad was from Jefferson Parish and was well aware of the accomplishments and expertise of Debra DePrato, who had started the first EBP in the state in Jefferson parish in 1996. Konrad knew firsthand of the successful outcomes of DePrato's programs and was familiar with high quality assessment and treatment practices.

At the time of the lawsuit Dr. Debra DePrato was serving on the faculty of the LSU Health Science Center, as well as running the Jefferson Parrish Human Services Authority, which was a pilot program combining mental and physical health services, the first of its kind in the nation and the first EPB in the state. A forensic psychiatrist with a degree from the Yale Medical School, Dr. Deprato had been trained in MST by Scott Henggeler and had experience in its implementation since 1994. This dedicated MST and EBP expert was running juvenile EBP programs right under the state bureaucrats noses in Jefferson Parish, a suburb of New Orleans. It was Judge Konrad who put the judicial foot down and declared that the court would enter a settlement agreement only under the condition that LSU would provide the services under the direction of Dr. DePrato who would head the reform efforts of the juvenile facilities involved in the law suit.

Based on her initial experience developing, staffing and implementing MST programs, Debra was strong in her conviction that she must maintain full control over all decisions from staffing to partnerships if this daunting reform effort were to have any chance at sustainability, let alone initial success. DePrato was adamant enough about the critical importance of maintaining local autonomy to negotiate terms with the Superior Court. Her response, therefore, was that she would take the job if she could do it on her own terms and with the full support of LSU in bringing the very best outside consultants and programs to assist with the reforms. A Consent Decree of sorts was initiated, which gave her the autonomy and authority to assess, develop, staff, and implement programs. Together with the United States Department of Justice, the state and private plaintiffs entered into a contractual settlement agreement addressing the multitude of issues raised in the lawsuits with Dr. DePrato and LSU in charge as the lead entity.

Prior to the law suit there was little knowledge about EBPs in Louisiana. Dr. Debra and her team in Jefferson parish were the only ones using them. MST was the only true EPB being used at the time. At Jefferson Parish Human Services

Authority they had MST, Competency Assessment and the Evaluation Program as official EBPs in place. DePrato describes how during the initiation process, as she was working unfunded, they may not have had the resources or funding to always use EPB programs, but how, "Everything we did was as close to EPB as possible," and the respect for outcome based and scientifically proven models was growing.

Dr. Deprato had learned the importance of maintaining local autonomy through her experience working with MST. Once she had been trained in MST and was ready for the selection and training of her staff, MST sent in their own experts to oversee her team. She saw right away that this would not work and insisted on training her own supervisory team, instead of having "an outside expert coming in and telling them what to do." She explained bluntly, "It just won't work," to have someone you don't know, come in from somewhere else and tell your staff what to do. She emphasizes the critical importance of having autonomy within your own state as they had, and ideally locally within communities, but also notes how she had to demand it to make it happen, both with her initial EBP experience and again in the settlement agreement when she demanded the same thing of the Louisiana Superior Court. Initially, MST Services experts were overseeing the Jefferson Parrish therapists. At that time MST did not allow providers to oversee their own program, sending in their own experienced experts instead. Debra decided that they needed a supervisory model based on their needs to train their own supervisors from within the organization.

Before being asked to take over health care in all the state's juvenile institutions, Debra served on the faculty as program director for LSU-HSU, which is an Accredited Division of Forensic Psychiatry, where she trained residents coming through the medical school program. As she built her program she picked people she had either trained as residents in Forensic Psychiatry or had worked with within the criminal justice field. She also made an intentional effort to know everyone around her, believing each person has a certain amount of influence within their circle of contacts and every position and every person matters.

6.3 Screening, Assessment and Tracking

The first step in overhauling the secure care facilities was a needs assessment. Debra insisted they screen every youth in every facility individually, one-by-one. There were 1,400, at the time; now down to 450. They started at the Baton Rouge facility, where Debra had begun her work. The kids were sent to that facility to get assessed and then sent to the appropriate facility according to the results of the assessment. If substance abuse turned out to be the main issue, they would remain in the Baton Rouge facility for treatment, since that was their specialty of care. If there were multiple or combinations of issues, which was often the case, (they would assess which was the most predominant, and send them to the best suited facility, but track them closely to see how they are doing and responding to the environment and the treatment.

Starting her medical career as an Emergency Room physician, DePrato places great emphasis on how you assess each patient and track the effects of treatment. If the results are not beneficial to the patient, you alter or change the treatment and track it again. DePrato believes the same principles apply to children and young adults in the juvenile justice system. Kids must be screened properly or they will have the wrong issue treated and be sent to the wrong facility. Their original issue will not be addressed and most likely will be exacerbated by the circumstances. Without the supports necessary to address the identifiable issues, the child will not improve and will most likely become a costly burden to society.

Emphatically stating how much she learned from MST, DePrato explains, "It's very methodical. It works the way my brain works," which, as a trained physician, is very analytical and diagnostic. As they moved forward with very little if any funding, even if not yet "in science," they always tried to use as close as possible to an EBP and the best they could find. Or they developed what they needed according to the philosophy and methods of EBPs, such as an EBP Screening Assessment Process they developed. "This is where it really began," according to Debra. "The Movement from one local EBP to statewide awareness…because every juvenile got assessed and sent to proper treatment," and the public suddenly saw the immediate difference it was making.

In 2005, in the midst of this already challenging task of assessing the entire juvenile population in the system, Hurricane Katrina hit, and Debra, like many other citizens of Jefferson Parish, lost her home to the storm. Never hesitating, letting no obstacle impede pursuit of their goal, and with more need than ever following the storm, Debra and the collaborative team at LSU pursued their efforts as the momentum continued to build towards their vision of juvenile justice reform. In fact, through the tragic conditions of Katrina, arose an EBP triumph. DePrato explains how Baton Rouge became the center of activity.

"No one could communicate," as her facility in Baton Rouge took every juvenile, from every facility and detention center, who had nowhere else to go. All communications were cut off. Most of the displaced youth were from New Orleans families—the most devastated region. "We couldn't get in touch with parents or find their families or foster care providers." They were displaced from their facilities and remained in the Baton Rouge facility for 6–9 months. "It's a big facility," she explained, and the population had significantly downsized since the settlement, so there were empty residential facilities and available beds. But still they had to provide cots in the gymnasium and they had to remain a secure facility, so staff had to go with them everywhere.

The nurses literally stayed for days after Katrina, without even a change of clothes or toothbrush. Many of the staff stayed and took care of the kids for weeks. "We just did all we knew how to do," DePrato explains as a matter of fact. "We wrapped our arms around each other and the kids… and did what we had to do. We took care of them and each other."

"Because of all the work that had been done, when Katrina hit we could see how strong we truly were," she reflects. "Through crisis sometimes you see the gaps in the system, but in our case it brought us together and highlighted our strengths." They had a great network. "I was so proud of the staff."

6.4 Governance and Infrastructure

Over time the partnership with the state became increasingly interdependent, as LSU needed the government's support and funding to move the work forward, and the state needed LSU's guidance, expertise, training and research in order to create and implement policy to support the mandated reforms. As successful outcomes resulted, the state also mandated funding in those areas, with the settlement agreement still over their heads and always driving them to follow the directive of the Lead Entity's work.

Throughout the years that the work of DePrato and her team were starting to show outcomes, the state was implementing policies that would support and mandate these changes for the entire juvenile justice system. Political champions added to this momentum creating the pivotal impetus through legislation and creating needed funding streams to address target areas for improvement. Associate Justice Catherine D. Kimball was one of the champions behind the Reform Act and Implementation Commission, and a pivotal impetus behind this radical change. Following her work on the Commission, she then became Chief Justice of the Louisiana Supreme Court in 2009. Governor Blanco was very pro juvenile justice and pushed for reforms as quickly as possible.

6.5 Juvenile Justice Legislation

In 2003, the state legislature passed what is widely considered to be the most important piece of juvenile justice legislation passed in Louisiana. Act 1225: The Juvenile Justice Reform Act of 2003 recognized that "… the lack of available alternatives within local communities is a significant factor in the over-incarceration of juveniles in such large correctional facilities." Act 1225 charged the state with the task of assisting in the "development and establishment of a community-based, school-based and regionally-based system," while providing an opportunity for local involvement in planning such interventions. Ultimately, Act 1225 provided a framework for reforming and restructuring Louisiana's juvenile justice system.

One of the most important provisions of the Act involved the creation of the Louisiana Juvenile Justice Implementation Commission (JJIC) as an oversight body to guide implementation. This landmark legislation also provided for community involvement and facilitated collaborations among state and local agencies and various stakeholder groups. The legislation also led to the closure of Tallulah, the state juvenile correctional center in Madison Parish. A year later in 2004, Act 555 established the Children and Youth Planning Boards to assist in the efforts legislated by Act 1225. In addition to seeing initiatives through, the state was also aware of the need to do more in communications, giving rise to the planning board implementation.

Local models of Children and Youth Planning Boards (CYPB), with the basic principles, guidelines, bylaws, make-up, and strategies were achieved in three judicial districts. Each judicial district was successful in the design of the planning board based on area needs and target issues. The LA MfC/CYPB Model was developed with support from Models for Change and LSU HSC and then adopted by the Children's Cabinet and promulgated throughout the state via trainings by local experts. This process demonstrates the collaborative efforts with state, local and outside agencies working together to disseminate information and education in support of a working model. Currently, local planning boards come together to report their findings to the CYPB, who then make recommendations to the Children's Cabinet based upon their findings.

Also in 2004, the Office of Youth Development (OYD) was separated from the Department of Public Safety and Corrections (DPS&C) by Executive Order, reflecting the new direction that reforms were taking and constituting a significant change both in legislature and in the state's overall thinking about juvenile justice. Act 1276 of 2004 codified the separation of Youth Services from DPS&C. This gave rise to future strategic opportunities by LSU to engage judges and district attorneys in exclusive juvenile justice perspectives towards issues of concern.

In December 2005, the Office of Youth Development (OYD), now a separate entity from the DPS&C, disseminated a 5 year strategic plan in collaboration with LSU and the Lead Entity, Youth Services Strategic Plan, all in alignment with the goals of DePrato and the LSU team in disseminating EBP's. The plan outlined reforms including additional funding for community-based services, changing the culture within the juvenile justice system, prioritizing family involvement, and the regionalization of services.

Further evidence as to the level of critical importance that juvenile justice reform had reached in Louisiana was provided when the Deputy Secretary's position, as head of the Office of Youth Development, was elevated to cabinet level, answering directly to the governor. Then, in 2008, the Louisiana Legislature passed Act 565, changing the name of the agency from Office of Youth Development to Office of Juvenile Justice (OJJ). The Office of Juvenile Justice is now a cabinet-level agency whose head, the Deputy Secretary, reports directly to the Governor of Louisiana.

Juvenile Justice Programs are run under both state and local jurisdictions depending on the region, and in some cases both concurrently. Under the direction of the Deputy Secretary, the Office of Juvenile Justice (OJJ) has policy oversight and support responsibilities for state programs for youth who are adjudicated delinquent, as well as any youth and their families ruled in need of services by courts of juvenile jurisdiction (FINS—Families in Need of Services). They are responsible for youth assigned to their care by the court system, either for supervision or custody in residential placement, or secure care. OJJ also provides services to youth under local court supervision. OJJ operates three 24-h secure facilities for males and one for girls.

The Office of Juvenile Justice (OJJ) is a cabinet-level agency whose head, the Deputy Secretary, reports directly to the Governor of Louisiana. OJJ is the principal state partner through which all state-level decisions, policies and programs must pass. OJJ oversees the Children's Cabinet, which is the entity over the Children's Youth Planning Board, to which all local planning boards report. There is a dynamic, interdependent relationship between OJJ and the Lead Entity, represented in the collaboration of LSU HSC together with Models for Change.

Debra DePrato, as the director of MfC and LSU HSC, works with her team to provide the most efficient, cohesive data to guide policy and legislative decisions, which will move their goals forward. As much as OJJ depends on the guidance and technical support of LSU and MfC, so does the Lead Entity depend on OJJ to implement legislation which will further support their work. This relationship has proved, thus far, to be mutually supportive to both sides. Of course, there are imperfections, as in any relationship, but over the years they have devised, implemented, as well as legislated strategies to support the sustainability of the relationship despite administrative changes or any other major change or upheaval politically so that the work may continue to move forward.

Through prevention and diversion programs, OJJ also serves youth in the community who are not involved in the system. The Community Services program provides probation and parole supervision, and coordinates both residential and non-residential treatment services for delinquent youth, as well as status offenders and their families. The agency participates in programs for the purchase of care and treatment of children taken into custody under the provisions of the Children's Code, pending adjudication, disposition, placement, or any or all of the above.

Act 565 directed the closure of a large-scale secure facility for juveniles, and the development of a comprehensive, time-sensitive plan to reduce the overreliance on secure incarceration and to implement community-based services to be provided throughout the state. Act 565 authorized the Juvenile Justice Reform Act Implementation Commission to develop a comprehensive plan to move the juvenile offenders currently housed at the large secure facility to regional youth centers with significantly lower populations and housing units not to exceed 12 youths.

In the meantime, the final Department of Justice inspection tours found the state youth corrections facilities to be in compliance with the components of the settlement agreement, and on May 1, 2006, the state was officially released from the DOJ litigation and oversight, thereby ending the settlement agreement and at the same time giving rise to the momentous reform about to be forged due to these initially coerced but now embraced and growingly supported reform efforts.

6.6 MacArthur Foundation's Models for Change Initiative

At about this time, as Louisiana's reform movement began to take shape and attain national recognition, it gained the attention of the John D. and Catherine T. MacArthur Foundation's Models for Change initiative, a national initiative that aimed to create replicable models for juvenile justice reform. In 2005 Laurie Guarduque, Director of the Models for Change (MfC) program for MacArthur traveled around Louisiana with Debra, conducting focus groups with various juvenile justice stakeholders, all of whom expressed interest in implementing "programs that work." It was on the basis of these focus groups, and their prior reform efforts, that Louisiana was selected as one of four Models for Change states, with Debra heading up the effort.

The Models for Change grant basically allowed her to "pick what you want to do" and MfC would fund and support it with Technical Assistance and outside expertise. As she knew absolutely everyone in the juvenile justice system by now, who had either worked for her at some point or been one of her residents at LSU Medical School, and since the state via OJJ was in full support, she had carte blanche and a dedicated army to back her up.

Eventually Debra and her team decided to initiate reforms in all three areas targeted by MfC: (1) expanding alternatives to formal processing and secure confinement; (2) increasing access to evidence-based services; and (3) reducing disproportionate minority contact with the juvenile justice system. They were the only MfC state to take on the expansion of EBPs.

In addition, the MfC initiative provided support for statewide efforts to ensure that work carried out at the local level through Models for Change was aligned with the state's goals for juvenile justice reform, thus establishing a collaborative relationship with the state entity. Sites or groups working towards improvements in these three areas were provided with a variety of assistance available from a number of national organizations and experts involved with MfC called the National Resource Bank.

Although the dramatic improvement in outcomes reflected in the data, beginning in 2006, the year when MfC began in Louisiana, may appear to show that MfC generated some pretty remarkable results with their initiative in Louisiana, this only partially true. The fact is Louisiana was chosen as an MfC state precisely because they were "poised for change," having already laid the groundwork and created the collaborative networks as part of the DOJ settlement agreement in 1998. With no discredit to the earlier reform efforts that were accomplished with little support or funding, the fact remains that Models for Change has made an immeasurable difference in Louisiana by bringing in funding and assisting their collaborative work.

As DePrato and her team met with various leaders, planning boards and stakeholders to learn their views on how to best utilize the MfC funding and TA, they would ask the question, "What is our ultimate goal in Louisiana?" The answer was resoundingly unanimous: keep kids out of the system entirely, but especially out of the deep end. Louisiana's goals were designed to be interdependent and build upon one another. Progress in one area, therefor, would benefit all three.

Louisiana was a unique MfC state because it was the only one to take on all three of MfC's Targeted Areas for Improvement (TAIs), not only as a state but as an expectation for local participants as well. Every program, every stakeholder, from Governor to parent had these three goals in mind. Questions aligned with the progress towards reaching their goals were included on the survey created to evaluate the programs' fidelity and keep them focused on the right goals. Taking on this monumental task meant raising Louisiana's expectations and being held accountable for the progress thereof. The three TAIs, as outlined by MfC, have come to be part of the reformed Louisiana attitude towards juvenile justice and are now becoming engrained in the state's cultural mindset. Although they do not serve as true goals per se, according to Dr. Stephen Phillippi of LSU HSC IPHJ, they are more like guidance tools or standards to keep all stakeholders, the public and the overall message of reform focused and on the same page. It gave them a shared language and a shared vision.

Goals more specifically aligned with the state's particular issues and challenges, have also been outlined by stakeholders to more closely match the strides made towards all of the state's challenges, as they worked towards total system overhaul. The TAIs, along with these specific goals, have inspired many programs, strategies and tools to be developed, including an array of training curriculum, to lend guidance to participants struggling with specific challenges.

6.7 MfC Target Areas of Improvement

1. *Expanding Alternatives to Formal Processing and Secure Confinement*: Their goal was to improve access to effective community-based programs and services that can serve as alternatives to formal processing (AFP) and secure confinement in the juvenile justice system. Successful results were originally envisioned in 2006 as "best practice models for local needs assessment and planning efforts, interagency collaboration, funding of community based services to youth and families". Progress was made on both local and state levels. One important outcome was the development of a local informal status offender model via the court system. Data has shown that the primary referral of youth into the juvenile justice system is via FINS, with the school system being the primary referral agency.
2. *Increasing Access to Evidence-Based Services*: The goal here was to increase the availability of scientifically supported community-level interventions and the use of sound screening and assessment practices that divert youth into those interventions. Louisiana adopted a multi-faceted approach to growing evidence-based practices (EBPs). This approach reflected the state's understanding and recognition of the challenges of sustaining long-term, system-wide movements towards EPBs. Results anticipated included prompt screening/assessment, wider range of evidence based programs, expanded funding opportunities, better outcomes for youth and families, and provider/system accountability.

EBP work in Louisiana focused on three areas: (1) Research-driven reforms and data-driven planning; (2) Stakeholder education and awareness and building a culture supportive of evidence-based practices; and (3) Strategic Implementation appropriate for local jurisdictions' target populations, resources, and needs.

Key stakeholders were engaged in the reform process though a specific series of strategies developed and guided by Dr. Deprato. The result is a network of local "experts" who have now become the trainers and guides, and serve as a replicable model for engaging all stakeholders. This developed "in state" expertise, as well as, created a platform of sharing experiences and working through important

Previously, LA MfC set forth as a goal, "improve the quality of and access to juvenile indigent defense for every young person who enters the juvenile justice system" with the result being "a permanent capacity for juvenile indigent defense training and professional development" in the area of Juvenile Indigent Defense. The National Juvenile Defender Center (NJDC) has served as the NRB lead on juvenile indigent defense for LA MfC. The technical assistance offered by NJDC partnering with the Lead Entity has provided the bridge toward a model juvenile indigent defense system. Over the past 2 years, two entities have been created which provide a permanent capacity for juvenile indigent defense in Louisiana: the LSU Law Juvenile Defense Clinic and the Louisiana Office for Juvenile Indigent Defense.

The LSU Law Clinic was awarded two LA MfC grants resulting in a standalone best practice juvenile defender clinic and the hiring of a full time faculty member at LSU Law Clinic. As part of the Model Juvenile Defense Clinic at LSU Law, a model curriculum was developed with NJDC input, after reviewing/visiting the best defender clinic models in the nation. As part of the Juvenile Defense Clinic at LSU, there is now a waiting list of students who desire to participate in the clinic; graduates have become both defenders and prosecutors to date. (Include recent discussions in creating new PH programs as well to answer the needs of EBP trained practitioners coming from local university programs.

LAPDB developed a strong juvenile infrastructure inclusive of all the above components aided by support from the NJDC. The office is now developed, and it is a vital and emerging component of Louisiana's defender community. As part of the technical assistance rendered by the Lead Entity and NJDC, recently a statewide juvenile indigent defense strategy session was developed to aid the Chief Public Defenders Office, juvenile defenders from around the state, and board members to develop a long-term vision and strategic plan for the healthy growth of juvenile indigent defense.

The Juvenile Defense Action Network (JIDAN) was launched in Louisiana and has been extremely successful. The Louisiana State Public Defenders Office has led JIDAN in Louisiana and incorporated JIDAN members in an advisory board toward the ongoing development of juvenile indigent defense in Louisiana and to institutionalize the processes/partners beneficial from the JIDAN partnerships. In addition, a JIDAN grant was made to Juvenile Regional Services (JRS) by LA MfC to support statewide writs and appeals and post-dispositional work in key areas of the state, thereby creating a model for both processes for all defenders to utilize.

During the past 2 years, the Lead Entity worked with the Supreme Court and local legislators in reviewing JJ Reform Act 1225, and the remaining work to be done. The creation of state detention standards and licensure was one item that was never accomplished. The Lead Entity worked closely with the Supreme Court in developing a study resolution for the Supreme Court Judiciary Task Force to study the need for these standards. The Lead Entity provided consultation and support over a year after the study resolution was passed, and coordinated consultant input. After the 1 year study resolution, the Lead Entity worked with the key stakeholders in developing model language for statutory development of Juvenile Detention standards, which passed the legislature unanimously in the spring of 2010. All detention centers must be licensed in best practice standards by January 2013 in Louisiana.

The Lead Entity engaged the Louisiana Juvenile Detention Association, and spearheaded the development of a LA MfC grant to support the development of these standards. The grant was awarded and work is underway to complete the work. At this time, the standards are developed and DCFS (the state licensure body) is working to create the process for licensure from the standards. The Lead Entity garnered extra support and Technical Assistance from the US DOJ for this process, which demonstrates the credibility of their work and of best practices and the DOJs support of them.

The Lead Entity was tasked with the development of a sustainable entity and home for the final phase of the LA MfC work. (The LA MfC grant was originally housed within the Louisiana Board of Regents). The Lead Entity in consultation with the Technical Assistance Collaborative, the Foundation, and the BOR, agreed that the best home would be in an academic setting. It was determined that the LSU HSC School of Public Health would house the Lead Entity administratively, and the physical location would be in the LSU Law Center. These moves were made over the course of the past 2 years. The next step was the development of an Institute proposal to be approved by the LSU Board of Supervisors and the BOR. The proposal was approved for the LSU HSC Institute for Public Health and Justice, with Dr. DePrato as the Director, and as the permanent home for the Louisiana LA MfC Lead Entity. The Institute has 2 full years to develop a plan for long-term funding and mission.

6.8 Outcomes and Accomplishments

Regarding their goal to expand and improve access to effective community-based programs and services that can serve as alternatives to formal processing and secure confinement in the juvenile justice system: Best practice models were developed for local needs assessment and planning efforts, interagency collaboration, and funding of community-based services to youth and families.

- Juvenile drug court triage, assessment, and treatment model.
- Status offender "system of care."
- Children and youth planning board model.
- Early intervention/diversion DA models.
- Local data show the number of youth formally processed in the JJ System has been reduced: 2006–2010: Referral of status offenders decreased by 40 % in Rapides and declined from the school system by 76 %.
- Formal adjudications dropped 55 % from 2006–2009 in Rapides.
- Youth processed by juvenile court decreased by 26 % over the past 4 years.
- Jefferson's adjudications for FINS dropped 15 % for informal and out of home placements for offenders fell 25 % without compromising public safety.
- Jefferson showed a 53 % reduction in status offender referrals.

Regarding their goal to increase the availability of scientifically supported commu- nity level interventions and the use of sound screening and assessment practices that divert youth into those interventions: they have provided prompt screening/ assessment, wider range of evidence-based programs, expanded funding opportu- nities, better outcomes for youth and families, provider/system accountability.

- Data driven decision making/measurable program outcomes.
- Evidence-based screening/assessment at key JJ decision points.
- DMC data collection/tracking/policy/interventions.
- Academic/public collaboration models.
- Juvenile justice data indicators at the state level.
- Information sharing models at local and state level.
- Best practice guidelines/recommendations for JJ professionals (DA/IDB/judiciary).
- Career development for JJ youth.
- In 2007, 19 % of youth involved in Jefferson Parish department of juvenile ser- vices were in EBPs, as compared to 2010 at 94 %.
- At the state level, 11 % of the programs and services were EBPs in 2007 as compared to 32 % of the programs and services as EBPs in 2011.
- Increase of 16 % in the utilization of research-based, standardized screening and assessment instruments over the course of 4 years.
- Increase of 27 % in the total youth served with evidence-based practices from 2007 to 2011.

Regarding their goal to improve DMC data collection where needed, develop capacity to collect and analyze DMC regularly at state and parish levels, use DMC data analyses and other research to identify, implement, and monitor appropriate interventions: They established a model DMC data collection and analysis capa- bilities at parish level that will lead to creation of evidence-based practices and other promising programs to address.

In addition to working to implement large scale evidence-based practices across Louisiana, Models for Change has, through the grant to the LSUHSC initiated a pro- fessional development strategy focused on building a foundation for evidence-based practices among a broad range of providers that may or may not have the capacity to undertake a large scale evidence-based program but could alter individual practices. LSUHSC developed and implemented a professional skills training for providers that includes motivational engagement of youth and families, cognitive-behavioral treatment, and social-ecological approaches to treating youth involved in the juve- nile justice system.

Since its' initial development 3 years ago, this training has reached hundreds of providers across the state through local and regional trainings, and workshops at state conferences, helping to ensure that youth in the care of Louisiana's providers are receiving services that are research-driven. Even more important, the development of in-state evidence-based practice training capacity, including the development of web-based learning technologies, at LSUHSC will help to ensure the sustainability and continued expansion of these practices long after the Models for Change efforts in Louisiana are completed.

Ensuring youth receive appropriate, evidence-based treatment requires that a youth's service needs be accurately identified. Given this, a major priority of the work over the past few years has focused on developing screening and assessment processes that rely on scientifically-sound instruments. Working with the National Youth Screening Assistance Project (NYSAP), the local Models for Change parishes have taken steps to strengthen their screening and assessment processes through the adoption of proven instruments, development of policies and procedures to ensure that screening and assessment results are administered and used properly, and establishment of referral procedures that ensure that youth are linked to appropriate services based on screening and assessment results.

These local advancements led to diffusion across the state. For example, the Louisiana Office of Juvenile Justice (OJJ) implemented the Structured Assessment of Violence Risk in Youth (SAVRY), a scientifically-sound violence risk assessment tool that can be used to guide service planning (Borum et al. 2006), in probation offices across the state. Implementation of the SAVRY began with a pilot project in Caddo Parish to implement a pre-dispositional assessment process. As part of the pilot project, Caddo Parish implemented the SAVRY and the Massachusetts Youth Screening Instrument (MAYSI-II) and pilot tested a "service matrix," developed through a collaboration between NYSAP, LSUHSC, and NCMHJJ, that is designed to guide service referral decisions based on SAVRY risk levels and identified needs. The SAVRY, along with region specific service matrices, are now in place statewide.

6.9 Lessons Learned

Why did some planning boards work and some didn't? It was an unfunded mandate. "Great idea, but no funding to support it," explains Phillippi and DePrato. People believed and pushed for it anyway. Some succeeded due to extra funding; some just because they really cared!!

The most important lesson learned from Louisiana's experience is the proven ability to overcome any obstacle or barrier. They have developed a strategy or approach for handling challenges as they occur, which has become an overall cultural perspective of embracing change. …a simple change of perspective turns it into an opportunity. The key players and stakeholders have proven this multiple times and have developed strategies to approaching various situations. Louisiana has developed an approach to facing barriers. They believe in the group approach and they collaboratively look at each obstacle and find a way to resolve it. This solutions-based thinking has garnered the official term Strategic Opportunities (SOs). Example of a Strategic Opportunity:

Obstacle: Can't get EBP. Reasons: doesn't fit needs of your region or organization, not available, limited or no funding available. What do you do?
Strategic Opportunity: to come together with your team, through the local planning board, and figure out what would work best based on your needs. Study other programs that have the qualities you desire and create your own, whether

it's a tool, strategy, method, or an entire program-it can be done! Issues encountered include assessment, evaluation, tracking, needs assessment, staffing, training, leadership, infrastructure, resistance, engaging partners and analyzing and utilizing data to move your goals forward. There are strategic models for each one as developed by Louisiana stakeholders and planning boards.

EBP vs. Best Practice or Outcome Based: Using "the best we could get" or "as close as possible" when you get EBPs. Developed data-driven accountability and evaluation measures, so only programs that meet certain requirements will be considered for referrals.

Leadership: Knowing your people; Giving your people credit; letting them take the credit and own the success. Build the leadership from within. Find and encourage your leaders in your community and organization. You must know everyone really well to be successful at picking and grooming leaders.

Know your people: You have got to know your people—all of them…every single one. Every single person and their role matters. One weak link can take the whole chain down or at least slow it up and affect the kids' care.

Lead Entity: Although there is no one person who did this, there is usually someone who is the driving force or impetus. This person or organization should become the Lead Entity. As DePrato clearly describes of her role, "My job is to make the work move on."

Collaboration: "The reason it (EBP) works in Louisiana is because it's a group effort. No one person did any of this," emphatically states DePrato. From local planning boards to OJJ's Children's Cabinet to the interdependent relationship between the state and local entities, universities, and partnerships, Louisiana has given a voice to each and every stakeholder while actively engaging and educating, at both community and state levels any who could have influence in moving their goals forward. Leave no stakeholder behind!

More DePratoisms:

Engagement through Empowerment: It's important to let people take credit and feel proud about what they've done. "Let them claim the credit; they've all earned it. Let them feel like the winner—they should," explains Debra Deprato. This is part of the Leadership piece, "building expertise" within your state or region. Everyone is an expert within their role. Let them own it!

The power of the referral: The referral process is critical. States DePrato, "People need to know how to refer, or it will kill the program." We have MST programs that just shut down because their own people, at the state level, didn't know how to refer.

Middle Management is everything: The critical, and often overlooked role of middle management, must be addressed. For example, we have someone in one of our parishes who is just "dragging their feet" in regards to substance abuse and mental health referrals. "You can't just work around them." And their boss at the state level didn't even know about it…didn't even know who they were! Answer to one local: So, what do you do…..this is what we are doing. You are either with it or you are not working here any longer. That's just how it is. That's how it has to be, because, "It's not easy. This work is hard. But it's so worth it."

Making it Happen: Demand the things you need. Find people, organizations, champions to support you. Put in place what pieces are necessary to solve the puzzle and make it all happen. Although each case, location, situation will vary there are only so many circumstances and there is a solution for each one that best expert to find it is YOU right in the middle of it because you know more and you know best than any outside expert. BUT you need their guidance to discover and create the right solution based on their past experiences and technical support. Be creative. Trust your thinking and intuition. Bring your people together to find the solutions. Let the leaders emerge and take credit.

There's always a way: When you hit a road-block in this work, you must just step back and think what needs to be done to overcome it and then make it happen.

Chapter 7
Pennsylvania, Washington, Florida and California: Helping or Letting it Happen

7.1 Pennsylvania: A Decentralized Early Starter

7.1.1 Overview

The development of evidence-based programs in the Commonwealth of Pennsylvania, also an early starter like Connecticut, followed along a somewhat different path. Unlike most other states, juvenile justice policy in Pennsylvania is largely controlled by the influential Juvenile Court Judges Commission (JCJC), which has experienced staff to serve its research and planning needs (see http://www.jcjc.state.pa.us/portal/server.pt/community/about_jcjc/5984).

Another state agency with experience in research and evaluation is the Pennsylvania Commission on Crime and Delinquency (PCCD), which controls most of the block grants that come to the state for criminal justice purposes (http://www.pccd.state.pa.us/portal/server.pt/community/pccd_home/5226). Both of these groups have had a long-term interest in improving outcomes for juveniles. Also, the state was one of the first to adopt Communities That Care (CTC) in the early 1990s. CTC is a planning system that helps guide communities through the steps of identifying needs and provides the best means of selecting evidence-based programs (Feinberg et al. 2010). The agency with the primary responsibility for assisting communities in selecting programs, implementation, fidelity measurement and outcomes is the Evidence-based Prevention and Intervention Support (EPIS) Center, located at Pennsylvania State University and supported by PCCD.

7.1.2 History and Development

The Commonwealth of Pennsylvania has a rich history, representing one of the first colonies and the hub of movement for independence from Great Britain. It has a large rural geographic area, but also boasts two major metropolitan cities,

P. Greenwood, *Evidence-Based Practice in Juvenile Justice*,
SpringerBriefs in Translational Criminology, DOI: 10.1007/978-1-4614-8908-5_7,
© The Author(s) 2014

Pittsburgh and Philadelphia. In terms of population size, according to the latest census data, there are *12,742,886 people living in the Commonwealth, which makes it large relative to other states (6th most populous state in the nation). It is also densely populated, with 447 people per square mile compared to only 87 for the national average.*

According to the Bureau of Labor Statistics, since 2011, the unemployment rate has held relatively steady, at around 7.7 %, which is lower than the national rate of 8.1 % (as of April, 2012). The poverty rate in Pennsylvania has mirrored the national rate over time in the last few years, but has remained roughly 3 % lower than the U.S. average (Pennsylvania Budget and Policy Center 2011).

Juvenile justice in Pennsylvania operates in a decentralized manner, which means that it does not administer services or control operations in particular jurisdictions. This is done on the county level, with the juvenile court judge in charge of decision-making (National Center for Juvenile Justice 2005). Children as young as 10 and as old as 20 years are eligible for juvenile justice services in the Commonwealth, with the maximum age generally capped at 17 years. Attention is paid to the principles of restorative justice at all stages of the system, with an end goal of fostering improved youth development. Juvenile courts are guided by the Juvenile Court Judges Commission. This Commission develops rules and regulations regarding sentencing and also advises courts on organizational issues (Commonwealth of Pennsylvania 2012).

There are 24 distinct juvenile detention centers across Pennsylvania that can hold nearly 800 individuals. Pennsylvania also has provisions for alternate sentencing or diversion from the formal justice system, including electronic monitoring, day reporting centers, and home confinement (NCJJ 2005). Probation officers are responsible for supervision and may oversee adults and juveniles. Probation officers are required to hold at least a Bachelor's degree with a focus on the social sciences.

7.1.3 The Early Days

Unlike our five leading states (Connecticut, Hawaii, Louisiana, Maine, and New Mexico), the move toward evidence-based programs in Pennsylvania did not begin with a lawsuit by the Department of Justice, a scandal, or concerns about number of juvenile placements. Rather, the spread of evidence-based programs in the Commonwealth can be seen as part of the natural evolution, continuation, and extension of the continuous "search for more effective programs" perspective that guided key juvenile justice stakeholders for decades. Pennsylvania policymakers had long recognized that many of the resources that were committed to the prevention of youth violence, delinquency, substance abuse, teen pregnancy, and educational failure had been invested in untested programs with little or no evaluation. This was why they were one of the first states to implement the Communities That Care (CTC) program as a way of helping local communities make better decisions about youth programing. It was also part of the reason one of the authors

(Greenwood) was able to test an experimental reentry program with a randomized controlled experiment in Pittsburgh (with VisionQuest implementing the program with a high degree of fidelity, and finding no impact on recidivism).

The funding to implement Blueprints programs in Pennsylvania was initially provided by a special fund established by then Governor Tom Ridge. Pennsylvania had been one of the sponsors of the Blueprints initiative that identified the model programs. Over time, this special funding for evidence-based programs was expanded to help other new programs get started (Yeager 2011). In recent years this special funding has been reduced so that EBPs have to find funding through state sources such as Medicaid, Probation, or Education. Nearly 200 EBPs have been funded by the state since 1998, with another 200 funded through other sources (Bumbarger 2011). The intermediary agency that has assisted counties in selecting, implementing and monitoring EBPs is the EPIS Center, located within the Pennsylvania State University Prevention Research Center (http://www.episcenter.psu.ed).

Again, unlike the leading five states, Pennsylvania did not restrict itself to implementing just a few models. It has been helping counties adopt the full range of Blueprints proven models. Today, the list of programs supported by the EPIS Center includes: Big Brothers/Sisters, Life Skills Training (LST), Strengthening Families Program (SFP 10–14), Promoting Alternative Thinking Strategies (PATHS), MST, FFT, MTFC, Olweus's Anti-Bullying Program, Project Toward No Drug Abuse (TND), and The Incredible Years. The EPIS Center has also helped standardize the collection, analysis, and reporting of performance measures, and helped to monitor implementation progress.

In meeting its public safety responsibilities, Pennsylvania's juvenile justice system has turned away from a purely reactive approach to delinquency in favor of one that focuses on creating conditions and programs that promote positive development for all young people and prevents delinquency from occurring in the first place. The community-based, risk-focused prevention approach to reducing delinquency they promote recognizes the limits of time and resources available to the court, and recruits schools, community organizations, businesses, and public agencies (both justice and service-related) to play a part in the work of preventing and reducing delinquency. They subscribe to the public health perspective that believes that successful delinquency prevention programs attempt to increase protective factors—those positive traits, beliefs, relationships, and connections in juveniles' lives that help them overcome adversity.

7.1.4 Key Players

7.1.4.1 Pennsylvania Commission on Crime and Delinquency (PCCD)

The PCCD was established in 1978 with the mission to improve the criminal justice system in Pennsylvania. Commission members bring a broad array of backgrounds and expertise and include judges, members of the legislature and the

Governor's administration, representatives of law enforcement, and victim service organizations, as well as private citizens.

Working closely with the Governor's office, the Commission helps coordinate the work of state and local criminal justice agencies to increase communication, effectiveness, and efficiency. PCCD provides training to deputy sheriffs and constables and technical assistance to communities and organizations to promote crime and delinquency prevention efforts. PCCD allocates federal and state funds to victims, victim service providers, criminal and juvenile justice, and ancillary agencies, and helps communities to improve the administration of justice in a variety of ways.

PCCD's Juvenile Justice and Delinquency Prevention Committee (JJDPC) serves as the State Advisory Group (SAG), which has the responsibility for guiding the expenditure of federal and state funds. To direct and unify the Commonwealth's juvenile justice system in adopting policies and practices consistent with the new purpose clause, JJDPC adopted the following mission statement: "Juvenile Justice: Community Protection, Victim Restoration, and Youth Redemption," as well as guiding principles to define best practices and shape policy decisions within the system:

• Community protection refers to the right of all Pennsylvania citizens to be and feel safe from crime.
• Victim restoration emphasizes that, in Pennsylvania, a juvenile who commits a crime harms the victim of the crime and the community, and thereby incurs an obligation to repair that harm to the greatest extent possible.
• Youth redemption embodies the belief that juvenile offenders in Pennsylvania have strengths, are capable of change, can earn redemption, and can become responsible and productive members of their communities (Juvenile Justice and Delinquency Prevention Committee 2004).

By statute, PCCD is required to prepare (and update every 2 years) a comprehensive juvenile justice plan based on an analysis of the Commonwealth's needs and problems, including delinquency prevention. JJDPC has been charged with developing this plan.

With support from PCCD's Juvenile Justice and Delinquency Prevention Committee (JJDPC), and PCCD funding, many communities across the Commonwealth have received training and support to identify risk factors and protective factors relative to adolescent problem behavior and implement prevention programs designed to reduce or eliminate risk factors and facilitate protective factors. The goal of PCCD funding is to support the implementation of programs proven to be effective in preventing and reducing a range of adolescent problem behaviors (e.g., violence, delinquency, substance abuse, educational failure, teen pregnancy) in communities, which are engaged in a collaborative risk-focused prevention planning process.

The 2003 Juvenile Justice and Delinquency Prevention Plan outlined the PCCD's research-based prevention initiatives, including Children's Partnership/Delinquency Prevention funding for CTC efforts and support for the implementation of proven

Blueprints programs and other model programs in Pennsylvania communities, and requested continued state funding of these initiatives.

7.1.4.2 Juvenile Court Judges Commission

The Pennsylvania Legislature established the Juvenile Court Judges Commission in 1959. Members of the commission are nominated by the Chief Justice of the Pennsylvania Supreme Court and appointed by the governor for 3-year terms. The commission is responsible for: (1) advising juvenile courts concerning the proper care and maintenance of delinquent and dependent children; (2) establishing standards governing the administrative practices and judicial procedures used in juvenile courts; (3) establishing personnel practices and employment standards used in probation offices; (4) collecting, compiling, and publishing juvenile court statistics; and (5) administering a grant-in-aid program to improve county juvenile probation.

The 2003 PCCD Plan recommended that the commission develop best practice standards regarding behavioral health screening, assessment, and evaluation of youth in the juvenile justice system. In response, the commission has focused on researching and identifying behavioral health screening and assessment instruments in cooperation with the Pennsylvania Council of Chief Juvenile Probation Officers. A sub-committee of this council dedicated to researching various screening and assessment instruments reviewed a large number of established instruments designed to screen and assess children's behavioral health needs, narrowing the list to six. Selected instruments from this short list will be piloted in several counties to determine their usefulness for the juvenile justice population.

7.1.4.3 The Evidence-Based Prevention and Intervention Support (EPIS) Center

The EPIS Center is funded by PCCD to support and advance the use of evidence-based programs; more specifically, the Center:

- Directs outreach and advocacy efforts to foster recognition, at federal, state, and community levels, of the value and impact of proven prevention and intervention programs.
- Provides technical assistance to communities to improve implementation quality, promote the collection and use of program impact data, and foster proactive planning for long-term program sustainability.
- Develops and provides educational opportunities and resources to disseminate current prevention science research and facilitate peer networking.
- Conducts original research to inform more effective prevention practice and the successful dissemination of evidence-based programs.

In supporting the needs of local communities in developing their own evidence-based program agendas, the EPIS Center currently finds its primary roles as providing syntheses and translation of research to practice (and practice to research) and helping local stakeholders with the following:

- Acquire and interpret community risk information, and choose appropriate programs.
- Ensure sufficient implementation quality and fidelity.
- Understand adaptation and preventing program drift.
- Measure and monitor implementation and outcomes.
- Address policy, systems, and infrastructure barriers.
- Coordinate across multiple programs and from a developmental perspective.
- Sustain programs in the absence of dedicated prevention infrastructure (Bumbarger and Perkins 2008).

Some of the specific policy and practice innovations attributed to the Center include: development and support of "communities of practice;" inclusion of common public health language in RFAs; statewide surveillance system that focuses on underlying causal mechanisms (compared to narrowly defined behavioral outcomes); support for community collaboratives as local prevention infrastructure; and ongoing monitoring of implementation. Figure 7.1 shows how the Center views its connections with all its key stakeholders.

EPIS staff also believe that although numerous evidence-based programs have been proven effective in research trials and are being widely promoted through federal, state, and philanthropic efforts, few have been "scaled-up" in a manner likely to have a measurable impact on critical social problems. Their Interactive Systems Framework for Dissemination and Implementation (ISF) explicates three systems they see as critical in addressing the barriers that prevent these programs from having their intended public health impact: (1) prevention synthesis and translation system; (2) prevention delivery system; (3) and prevention support system (Rhoades et al. 2012).

In addition to its role in supporting the spread of Blueprints programs, the EPIS Center also assists communities in documenting and improving the effectiveness of what it calls "practice based" programs (see Fig. 7.2). Along these lines, one

Fig. 7.1 Prevention support system as infrastructure

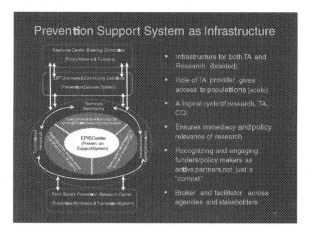

Fig. 7.2 Evidence-based programs compared to practice-based programs

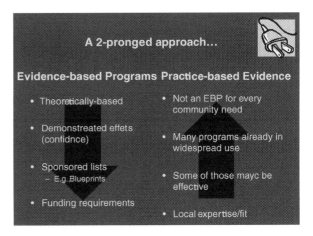

county in the Commonwealth was selected to participate in pilot testing the use of Mark Lipsey's Standardized Program Evaluation Protocol, which provides a means of rating, and hopefully improving, the effectiveness of generic based programs (Lipsey et al. 2010).

7.1.5 Partnerships and Governance

In addition to the efforts of the EPIS Center, JCJC, and PCCD, there are other key players helping to push juvenile justice in the Commonwealth in a positive direction. The Commonwealth is one of four leading states that participated in the MacArthur Foundation's "Models for Change Project." The others are Washington, Louisiana, and Illinois. "Models for Change" is a national initiative designed to accelerate reforms of juvenile justice systems across the country. Focused on efforts in select states, the initiative aims to create replicable models for reform that effectively hold young people accountable for their actions, provide for their rehabilitation, protect them from harm, increase their life chances, and manage the risk they pose to themselves and to public safety. The initiative emphasizes evidence-based practices and provides support to the states to develop, implement, and sustain lasting reform (see http://www.modelsforchange.net/index.htm).

Pennsylvania is also a member of the Mental Health/Juvenile Justice Action Network, whose goals are to establish a leadership community of states that will forge and implement new strategies for better identifying and treating youth with mental health needs involved with the juvenile justice system. The Network is organized around four key objectives:

1. Foster the development and exchange of ideas among the Network states. Activities include conference calls, teleconference calls on key topics, use of the Action Network website, and network cross-state site visits.

2. Support and enhance the progress already underway within each of the Network states by providing information, resources, and expertise. Activities include developing state strategic action plans to address an identified topic and implementing the strategic plans, with technical assistance provided as necessary.
3. Develop and implement new strategies and solutions to common problems. Activities include identifying strategic innovation topics, designating representatives to serve on Strategic Innovation Groups (SIGs), implementing the SIG recommendations, and tracking resulting changes.
4. Provide national leadership on mental health and juvenile justice. Activities include convening a national leadership forum, conducting national conference presentations, producing publications to document the Network's experiences and findings, and serving as host sites to visiting states and communities.

The partner states were all selected using a highly competitive application process based on objective criteria. Anticipated outcomes include: (a) creation of a learning network resulting in the accelerated sharing and implementation of effective policies and practices; (b) concrete improvements within the Network states for the identification and treatment of justice-involved youth with mental health problems; (c) development and implementation of innovative strategies to address critical mental health and juvenile justice issues confronting states; and (d) establishment of a leadership community that will shape the nationwide response for addressing the needs of youth with mental health issues in contact with the juvenile justice system.

Still other key players are crucial to promoting EBP in the Commonwealth. One of these is the Center for Juvenile Justice Training and Research (CJJTR), which was established by the Juvenile Court Judges Commission at Shippensburg University in 1982. CJJTR provides higher education opportunities and professional development primarily for juvenile probation officers. Its graduate education program provides a 2-year masters program for which tuition is underwritten by JCJC. The Center also provides annual professional development.

In September 2003, an executive order by the Governor created the Cabinet on Children and Families. The Cabinet's purpose is to recommend to the Governor ways to improve the delivery of services to children and families by making the services more responsive, efficient, and effective. The Cabinet's 11 members include the secretaries of Public Welfare, Education, Health, and Labor and Industry; the Secretary of the Budget; the Insurance Commissioner; the directors of the Office of Health Care Reform and the Governor's Office of Policy; the Governor's Chief of Staff; and the chairpersons of the JCJC and PCCD.

The Juvenile Law Center (JLC) is one of the oldest children's rights organizations in the country. Founded in 1975 as a non-profit legal service, JLC works on behalf of children who have come within the purview of public agencies. These include abused or neglected children placed in foster homes, delinquent youth sent to residential treatment facilities or adult prisons, or children in placement with specialized services needs. Although JLC primarily serves the children of the

Commonwealth, the Center is often asked to lend their expertise to national child advocacy efforts.

The Pennsylvania Alliance for Children and Families (PACF) is an educational advocacy organization for agencies that serve children and families across Pennsylvania. PACF advocates for resources and policies that strengthen family life; educates policymakers about services for families; and engages in activities that help member agencies provide needed and quality services to local families.

The Pennsylvania Association of Probation, Parole, and Corrections (PAPPC) is a professional association open to all juvenile and adult criminal justice practitioners in the Commonwealth. Its objectives include: advancing methods and standards in the field of juvenile and adult probation, parole and institutional care; promoting appropriate legislation; and cooperating as much as possible with progressive treatment and prevention strategies (see http://www.pappc.org/).

The Pennsylvania Council of Chief Juvenile Probation Officers began over 30 years ago as a membership organization of chiefs, deputy chiefs or assistant chiefs, and supervisors of juvenile probation departments (see http://www.pachief probationofficers.org/). Juvenile probation officers can be associate members. The Council takes an active role in sponsoring legislation on juvenile justice-related topics, recommending training topics for the Center for Juvenile Justice Training and Research, and working closely with the Juvenile Court Judges Commission. The Council is organizing a national network of Chief Associations.

The Pennsylvania Partnerships for Children (PPC) is an advocacy organization that works to promote the well being of children throughout the Commonwealth (see http://www.papartnership.org/). Focusing on early care and education, child health, and family support, PPC develops policy proposals that are based on and supported by statistical and research findings.

7.1.6 Funding

The state and county share costs not otherwise covered by federal or private sources. Counties bear the largest financial burden since they are almost solely responsible for the provision of probation services, the most common service provided to delinquent youth in the Commonwealth. Counties purchase other juvenile justice services, such as in-home services, community-based placements, and institutional placements, with the state providing reimbursement. For more than 35 years the funding mechanism created by Act 148 (1976) has set reimbursement rates at varying levels depending on the kind of services and the setting in which they were provided. State reimbursement is capped with each county allocated a finite amount, determined through the "unified needs-based budgeting process," to draw upon each year for services to dependent and delinquent children and youth. The county is liable for actual expenditures that exceed the cap. Act 148 and needs-based budgeting have profoundly changed both the character of delinquency services and the way they are delivered in Pennsylvania. This strategy has

Fig. 7.3 Some concrete
examples: funding
requirements

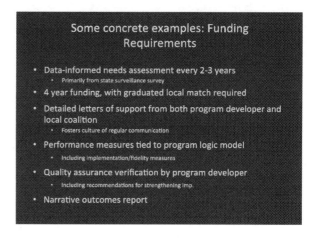

served as a model in other states and was featured as one "keystone for reform" by the MacArthur Foundation. Figure 7.3 lists some of the specific program funding requirements that are not tied to direct services for youth.

7.1.7 Outcomes

Over the last decade, the Pennsylvania Commission on Crime and Delinquency has made a considerable investment in supporting community delinquency and crime prevention through the funding of proven programs under the state's Research-based Programs Initiative. These evidence-based prevention programs, implemented in over 120 communities throughout the Commonwealth, have been shown in rigorous evaluation studies to reduce delinquency, violence and aggression, drug and alcohol use, and other youth behavior problems, and to promote positive youth development and stronger families and communities. Figure 7.4

Fig. 7.4 Total number of
family based EBP by year

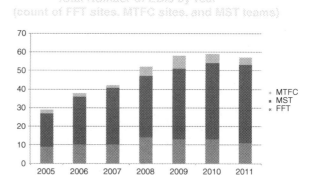

Pennsylvania's EBP dissemination in 2012...

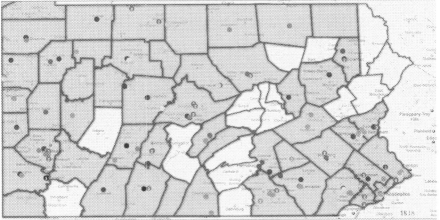

Fig. 7.5   Distribution of blueprint programs across counties

shows the growth in the number of sites that have implemented one of the Blueprint family intervention programs.

Figure 7.5 shows the distribution of Blueprint programs across all counties in Pennsylvania, and Fig. 7.6 shows the number of counties that have adopted at least one EBP.

Figure 7.7 shows that the percentage of youth in placement declined in those counties adopting at least one EBP, but increased in those adopting none. Figure 7.8 uses court placements rates to show the steady decline in placements among counties adopting an EBP, compared to the increase in those not adopting an EBP.

Fig. 7.6   Number of counties with at least one EBP

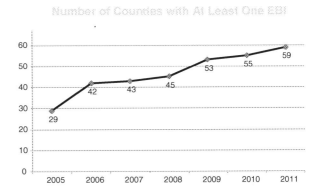

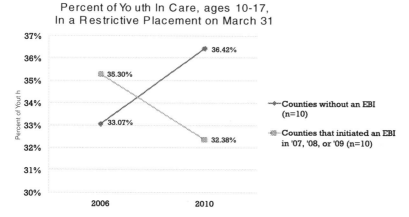

Fig. 7.7   Impact on youth placements (Bumbarger et al. 2010)

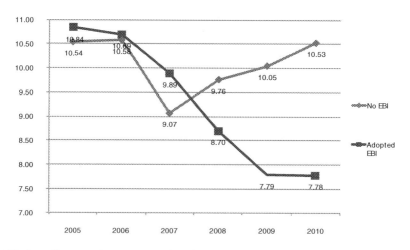

Fig. 7.8   Juvenile court placement rates (Bumbarger et al. 2010)

In a recent report, that examines the return-on investment for seven research-based programs that are supported by the PCCD, analysts at the EPIS Center, using conservative and widely-accepted methodology, determined that these programs not only pay for themselves, but represent a potential $317 million return to the Commonwealth in terms of reduced corrections costs, welfare and social services burden, drug and mental health treatment, and increased employment and tax

Cost-effectiveness of Evidence-based Prevention in PA
(measured benefits and costs per community and statewide)

Program	B-C per youth	Avg. Return/ Community	# Programs Statewide	Est. Total PA Return
Big Brothers/Sisters	$54	$13,500	28	$378,000
LifeSkills Training	$808	$161,600	100	$16,160,000
Multi. Treatment Foster Care	$79,331	$475,986	3	$1,427,958
Multisystemic Therapy	$16,716	$2,507,400	12	$30,088,800
Functional Family Therapy	$32,707	$12,395,953	11	$136,355,483
Nurse-Family Partnership	$36,878	$4,782,976	25	$119,574,400
Strength. Families	$6,541	$872,133	15	$13,082,000
TOTAL				$317,066,641

Jones, D., Bumbarger, B., Greenberg, M., Greenwood, P., and Kyler, S. (2008). The Economic Return on PCCD's Investment in Research-based Programs: A Cost-benefit Assessment of Delinquency Prevention in Pennsylvania.

Fig. 7.9   Cost-Effectiveness of Evidence-Based Prevention in PA

revenue (see Fig. 7.9 for details). The programs described in their report produce returns of between $1 and $25 per dollar invested, and can generate cost savings as great as $130 million for a single program (Jones et al. 2008).

A cross-sectional quasi-experimental study of 98,000 students in 147 PA communities found that youths in CTC communities reported lower rates of risk factors, substance use, and delinquency than youth in similar non-CTC communities; seven times as many as could be expected by chance (Bumbarger 2011). Communities using EBPs showed better outcomes on twice as many risk and protective factors and behaviors (14 times as many as by chance). The study used propensity score matching to minimize potential selection bias. The EPIS Center estimated that the 3,345 youth enrolled in supported EBPs saved Pennsylvania taxpayers approximately $4.5 million in placement-related costs alone (Bumbarger 2011).

7.1.8   Lessons Learned

A number of key lessons have been learned by the EPIS Center that hold relevance to the advancement of EBP across the state. These include:

- Dissemination of EBPs is a means rather than an end. The end goal is to improve outcomes for youth.

- Dissemination and high-quality implementation are often at odds because so many communities want to adapt the available models.
- Scale-up is different than dissemination and requires a different approach.
- The absence of prevention infrastructure is the root of all evil. It has to be in place for scale-up to work.
- Neither prevention science nor EBPs fill a vacuum.
- Some balance between evidence-based practices and practice-based evidence is required to engage communities.
- Intentional behavior change model—from extrinsic to intrinsic motivation—from a culture of compliance to a culture of excellence. Demonstrate, experience, build capacity, and increase a sense of efficacy.
- Greater focus on understanding, communicating and educating on logic models and theory of behavior change.
- The Commonwealth's balanced approach of evidence-based programs and practice-based evidence (local innovation) has been crucial.
- CTC as an "operating system" for prevention infrastructure at the community level was critical to addressing the specific barriers to moving from lists to public health impact (EBPs are not an end in and of themselves, but a means to achieving the goal of public health impact measured at the population level).
- Again considering an explicit goal of moving practitioners from extrinsic (regulatory) to intrinsic motivation to measure and monitor implementation quality.

7.2 Washington State: By the Numbers

7.2.1 Overview

In Washington State, evidence-based programming and practice for delinquent youths began and continues with research. This research is rigorous, comprehensive, and constantly updated. It seemingly underlies all facets of the state's evidence-based initiative in juvenile justice (the focus here), adult criminal justice, and prevention. Uniquely, a major focus of the research program is on the monetary costs and benefits of programs and how savings accrue to government and taxpayers.

Many other features of the state's evidence-based juvenile justice initiative stand out. The initiative was authorized by statute—the Community Juvenile Accountability Act—in 1997. A single state agency, the Juvenile Rehabilitation Administration, in partnership with county juvenile courts, has the mandate for administering funding. Risk assessment (to ensure programs are matched with the level of risk and treatment needs of youths) and quality assurance (to ensure fidelity to the model) are closely linked to the implementation and delivery of the programs. Over time, the initiative has nurtured strong working relationships among all concerned stakeholders and across the state with a deep commitment to deliver evidence-based programs to reduce juvenile offending. The latest research shows that between 25 and 30 % of eligible youths are participating in evidence-based programs and, importantly, the initiative is reducing juvenile crime and lowering costs to taxpayers in the state. Washington is in the second tier of states, when it comes to availability of EBPs, only with Pennsylvania and Colorado.

7.2.2 Introduction

Washington, in terms of geographic size, is the 18th largest state in the nation. The capital, Olympia, is located on the western edge of the state, roughly 300 miles from the city of Spokane, on its eastern border. There were 6,724,540 people living in Washington State as of the 2010 census, which is about 2 % of the total U.S. population. This population ranks Washington as the 13th largest state in the U.S., between Virginia and Massachusetts. Washington has been a relatively progressive state, allowing women the right to vote in 1910.

Juvenile justice in Washington is based on the decentralized model. The state manages certain portions of the system (e.g., prisons, parole) and counties administer other parts of the system (e.g., courts, probation). County courts are charged with administering justice services in most of Washington. For juveniles, judges utilize a determinate sentencing system in a presumptive framework. Juveniles can be waived to adult court for a variety of reasons, including discretionary waivers and statutory exclusions. Juveniles are also eligible for diversion if they commit a misdemeanor as a first time offense. Diversion is based upon a restorative justice approach. The most serious juvenile offenders are handled by Washington's Juvenile Rehabilitation Administration.

In the 1990s, rising prison rates and an increased sense of unsustainability of the system led to the experimentation with alternatives. First, in 1995, Washington tested a model of intensive probation. Initial research findings pointed to this practice as being ineffective. Then, in 1997, Washington passed the Community Juvenile Accountability Act, which authorized the use and evaluation of evidence-based practices as a method to reduce crime and costs to the state.

Washington State's experience with evidence-based practice has a fairly long history. In 1995, intensive probation was implemented across the state in an effort to deal with a growing population of juvenile offenders. Early results indicated that this program was largely ineffective in reducing juvenile recidivism (Drake 2008). Soon after, in 1997, the state legislature took a major step in the process toward developing a culture of evidence-based practice. It was that year that the legislature passed the Community Juvenile Accountability Act (CJAA). In fact, as reported by the Washington State Institute for Public Policy (2010a, p. 1), the ineffectiveness of the intensive juvenile probation program was "the impetus for the act." This act set out to "reduce crime, cost-effectively, by establishing 'research-based' programs in the juvenile court" (Drake 2008, p. 4).

7.2.3 The Community Juvenile Corrections Act

The CJAA was one of several initiatives across the nation seeking to increase the use of evidence-based practices to address juvenile offending. This included the "Blueprints" program at the University of Colorado at Boulder. The process these initiatives embraced involved selecting programs that had shown effectiveness in rigorous evaluations in multiple settings. The CJAA first created a committee, known as the CJAA Committee, to guide the efforts of the state in selecting and implementing programs. The need for sound research on what works and saves money was central to the selection of programs. (A separate section below describes the nature of the research and the main research centers involved.) Based on the research carried out by the Washington State Institute for Public Policy (WSIPP), four programs were selected for implementation: Functional Family Therapy (FFT), Multisystemic Therapy (MST), Coordination of Services (COS), and Aggression Replacement Training (ART). A fifth research-based program, Family Integrated Transition (FIT), has since been selected for use by juvenile courts (Wirschem 2011).

Also crucial was the need to link the research-based programs with risk assessments of the juveniles coming before the courts. Early on there was recognition for the need to test the various risk instruments in use; that is, to investigate if they were valid in assessing risk on a number of important dimensions, including the level of risk (i.e., low, moderate, or high) and the nature of the risk (e.g., delinquency, substance abuse, mental health). Indeed, the CJAA mandated the use of risk assessment for the assignment of youths to the various programs. In 1997, the WSIPP joined with the Washington Association of Juvenile Court Administrators to develop what became known as the "Washington State Juvenile Court Assessment." Implementation of the juvenile court assessment began in 1999.

Also important was that the evidence based programs were implemented with fidelity to the model; that is, the programs were implemented in a way that helped to ensure similar effectiveness to the original study. This was imbedded in the language of the CJAA, and a quality assurance steering committee was established. The steering committee is comprised of juvenile court staff representing various ranks and geographic regions, program experts, and regional consultants (Drake 2008, p. 9), and includes representatives from the Juvenile Rehabilitation Administration and the juvenile courts. The committee is involved in the development of quality assurance plans for all evidence-based programs (Phelps 2011). According to the FFT plan, "Ensuring model fidelity in a community based system of care requires an ongoing systematic system of both quality assurance and quality improvement" (CJAA Committee 2010, p. 1).

7.2.4 Research Centers

Four main research centers located in the state make substantial contributions to the research base for evidence-based practice in Washington State. The centers are: Washington State Institute for Public Policy; the Washington State Center for Court Research; the Seattle Social Development Group at the University of Washington; and Department of Psychiatry and Behavioral Science at the University of Washington.

7.2.4.1 Washington State Institute for Public Policy

The Washington State Institute for Public Policy (WSIPP) is an integral player in the evaluation and use of evidence-based practices in the state. WSIPP serves as the main research arm for the Washington State legislature, focusing on conducting objective research to determine the effectiveness of a variety of programs in the state. The Institute was created in 1983 and involves important stakeholders from education, the legislature, and the state executive office, and is also directly affiliated with Evergreen State College, located in Olympia. WSIPP not only conducts research to evaluate criminal justice programs and policies, but also examines child and adult services, mental health, education, teenage pregnancy, substance abuse, housing and other governmental issues (Aos 2011). The Institute's 16 board members include legislators, academics, and administrative members of the University of Washington and Evergreen State College.

With respect to juvenile justice, WSIPP has made a name for itself by developing and disseminating a cost-benefit analysis model as well as conducting high quality evaluations of evidence-based practices. The cost-benefit approach can be traced to the work of Steve Aos and colleagues (Washington State Institute for Public Policy 1998). In the mid-1990s, the Washington legislature tasked the WSIPP to evaluate juvenile as well as adult programs in the interest of saving resources and reducing recidivism. This directive was based on the passage of the Community Juvenile Accountability Act (CJAA), which sought to prevent juvenile crime through the use of evidence-based programs. This was the "nation's first statewide experiment of research-based programs for juvenile justice" (Barnoski 2004b, p. 1).

In response to the CJAA, WSIPP reviewed the national scholarly literature on evaluation programs, recommended certain programs, and then helped to evaluate those programs once implemented. In addition, WSIPP developed a cost-benefit tool to determine if program benefits outweigh program costs. The cost-benefit tool takes into account the costs of crime, in terms of courts, corrections and police activities that must react to and address such behavior. It then compares this to the costs of particular programs to determine if they result in a benefit to the taxpayer.

One of the more valuable aspects of the WSIPP's cost-benefit research is that the findings are conveyed in straightforward and meaningful metrics. For example, a recent report issued by the Institute reported that Functional Family Therapy (FFT) and Aggression Replacement Training (ART) are effective in reducing crime and produce substantial cost-savings to society. The analysis found that FFT reduces recidivism by as much as 18 % and for every dollar spent on FFT programming, $10.29 is saved in costs associated with crimes. For ART, recidivism was reduced by 9 % with a dollar cost-benefit of $10.58 (Drake et al. 2009).

To return to an earlier point, the Institute has also been responsible for evaluating a number of evidence-based programs in the state. Based on their cost-benefit work, which served as the basis for the selection of the original four evidence-based programs (FFT, ART, MST, and COS), it was important to investigate if these programs worked in the "real world" setting of Washington State. A summary report concluded that of the three programs that could be evaluated at the time (MST could not be evaluated because of implementation problems), all were highly effective and cost-beneficial (Barnoski 2004b). It was also determined that these results held up when the programs were "competently delivered," a point that further added to the on-going work in the state on quality assurance.

Most recently, the WSIPP has contracted with the Pew Center to construct a tool to allow states to assess programs that can save money and reduce crimes. Their work in refining the tools is ongoing and a "constant work in progress" (Washington State Institute for Public Policy 2010b, p. 2). Thus, the WSIPP represents an invaluable resource for the state of Washington and the nation at-large, providing much needed information in an open and translatable format which can be readily used by policy-makers and interested stakeholders.

7.2.4.2 Washington State Center for Court Research

The Center for Court Research became involved in assessing the work of Washington's Juvenile Courts in 2008, when it received an initial grant from the MacArthur Foundation to support development of two information resources, the Court Contact and Recidivism Database (CCRD) and the Assessments Research Database (ARD). The CCRD provides a person-level record of involvement with Washington's courts on matters related to dependency (as with children in foster care), status offending (as with children who are brought into court on a school-filed truancy petition) and juvenile delinquency or adult criminal offending. The CCRD allows tracking court contact, recidivism, and desistance across the life course, and is used to assess whether juvenile offenders who are released from court supervision, or from confinement with a state juvenile facility, return to court for new offenses. The ARD is a collection of data recorded at the person level that contains both the results of risk-level screening and the information collected from administration of the Washington Juvenile Court Assessment. For youth under probation supervision and receiving evidence-based interventions, the Assessment is typically administered before assignment to an evidence-based program, at intervals throughout probation supervision, and after the conclusion of treatment. In combination, the CCRD and ARD are now enabling a variety of measures of program reach and effectiveness, including measures of whether juveniles who are eligible for evidence-based treatment, based on their risk and needs, are assigned to treatment, whether assigned youth who start treatment complete treatment, and the effect of treatment on attitudes, behavior, and cognition. Matching ARD data with CCRD data permits measurement of recidivism rates during the post-supervision period.

In 2011, the Center began working with Washington State Aggression Replacement Training to develop a web-based data tool that supports collection of information about youth assignment to treatment, session attendance for youth in treatment, and information about the treatment provider. The new data source will be used to assess the relationships among provider characteristics, client characteristics, and outcomes, as well as to examine influences on engagement and retention in treatment.

7.2.4.3 Seattle Social Development Group, University of Washington

The Seattle Social Development Group (SSDG) is a working partnership that has also played a significant role in the widespread use and support of evidence-based programs in Washington. Their mission is to "understand and promote healthy behaviors and positive social development among diverse populations by:

- conducting research on factors that influence development
- developing and testing the effectiveness of interventions
- studying service systems and working to improve them
- advocating for science-based solutions to health and behavior problems
- disseminating knowledge, tools, and expertise produced by our research" (see www.sdrg.org).

The SSDG includes members from numerous disciplines, including criminology and social work. The group provides research assistance to other professionals at the University of Washington. Currently, SSDG is housed within the University of Washington's School of Social Work. The Survey Research Division (see http://www.sdrg.org/srd/) helps with research design, survey construction, and implementation. The Survey Research Division boasts an Integrated Data Collection System (IDCS), which facilitates the administration and collection of surveys through telephone, mail, and the Internet. SSDG has been instrumental in building the base of evidence to address juvenile delinquency and other problem behaviors.

Two major projects help to illustrate the contributions SSDG has made to evidence-based practices. Perhaps the most well-known study that the SSDG is engaged in is the Seattle Social Development Project (SSDP), under the leadership of J. David Hawkins and Richard C. Catalano. The SSDP began as an academic study of the development of problem behaviors, which was initiated in 1981. The main thrust of the study was to assess the effectiveness of a multi-factorial program that included teacher and parent training, as well as child skill development. First grade children (n = 500) were randomly assigned to an intervention or a control group. The study was then expanded in 1985, including more youth (n = 808) who were in fifth grade, and their teachers as well as parents. In the fifth grade sample, schools were assigned (without randomization) to the intervention or control group (Hawkins et al. 2005, 2010). The study has assessed not only criminal behavior, but also substance abuse, truancy, and school drop-out.

The SSDP has contributed much knowledge about the risk and protective factors associated with delinquency and problem behaviors. The risk factors the project has isolated are generally collapsed into five groups: (1) community factors (disorganization, poverty); (2) family factors (poor parental management, harsh discipline, low bonding); (3) school factors (academic difficulty, low bonding); (4) peer factors (peers engaged in problem behaviors); and (5) individual factors (personality traits, favorable attitudes toward antisocial behavior).

As a result of the information learned from the SSDP, the SSDG has been able to develop and implement interventions that seek to promote healthy behaviors and prevent the emergence of risk factors. The Communities that Care (CTC) intervention is based upon these principles. CTC is a locally-driven approach to prevention of delinquency and other problem behaviors. It involves organizing leaders from the community to identify needs as well as appropriate evidence-based practices to implement. The process also heavily emphasizes evaluation to ensure that the strategies chosen actually work. The main organizing theme of CTC is to promote "bonding" with pro-social institutions (Hawkins 1995).

Thus far, CTC has been examined in two rigorous studies. The first, in Pennsylvania, involved a comparison of 120 communities utilizing CTC to a group of communities without the program. The results, as reported by the SSDG, indicated that the CTC communities had significantly fewer problem behaviors than the control communities. A second study involved a multi-state evaluation of CTC. Once again, data indicated that the program significantly reduced delinquency and other problem behaviors (Hawkins et al. 2010). A recent cost-benefit analysis of CTC effects on delinquency and smoking at eighth grade showed that for every dollar spent on the program between $5.30 and $10.23 are saved to society (Kuklinski et al. 2012).

7.2.4.4 Department of Psychiatry and Behavioral Sciences, University of Washington

Another major player in developing the culture of evidence-based practices in Washington is the Department of Psychiatry and Behavioral and Social Sciences, located at the University of Washington, School of Medicine. The department assists the state legislature in conducting research and implementing evidence-based practices in the area of child mental health. It is a very large department, with 250 regular and 400 "volunteer faculty," and receives over $30 million in grant funding, on average, per year (see http://www.uwpsychiatry.org/).

Importantly, with respect to assisting the state in its research efforts regarding juvenile justice are several institutes that are connected to the department. The Evidence-Based Practice Institute provides information and resources for evidence-based practices. In addition, the Division of Public Behavioral Health and Justice Policy (PBHJP) is a part of the department. The division was created in 1982, as part of an effort to ensure that qualified and talented mental health professionals remain in the state. Since then, the division has assisted the legislature with research on public health issues. The division is also important in helping implement programs that require clinical specialists (see http://depts.washington.edu/pbhjp/).

7.2.5 Risk Assessment

As noted above, the assessment of juvenile offenders' risk for reoffending is closely linked with the implementation of evidence-based programs in the state. The "Washington State Juvenile Court Assessment," first used in the juvenile courts in 1999, serves three major functions: (1) to measure risk factors for offending as well as protective factors against offending; (2) to classify youth as low, moderate, or high risk for reoffending in the community; and (3) to screen youth for program eligibility (Drake 2008, p. 6). It has an explicit aim of helping the courts "guide the rehabilitative effort," and its process can be summarized as follows: "A case management plan is developed that focuses on intervention strategies linked to reductions in future criminal behavior by reducing "risk" factors … and strengthening "protective" factors (such as effective interpersonal skills). Courts target more intensive efforts toward higher-risk youth" (Washington State Institute for Public Policy 2010, p. 2).

Following the implementation of the risk assessment, research was conducted by the WSIPP to assess its validity. Barnoski (2004a) found that the overall validity of the pre-screen portion of the assessment—the first stage that is administered to all youth on probation and indicates the risk for re-offending (low, moderate, or high)—was "good and typical of assessments in the literature". The full assessment, which is required only for those youth found to be at moderate or high risk on the pre-screen, serves to identify risk and protective factors to aid in planning treatment. Barnoski (2004a) also found that the full assessment is valid, concluding that, "it is appropriate for the courts to use the assessment to assign youth to programs designed to address a youth's risk profile and to expect that effective programs will reduce risk and increase protective factor scores" (p. 1).

7.2.6 Quality Assurance and Improvement

Both quality assurance and quality improvement play an integral part in the implementation and day-to-day delivery of evidence-based programs in the state. Quality assurance is defined as the "ongoing and accurate monitoring and tracking of reliable measures of model implementation." Quality improvement is defined as the "systematic implementation of activities to improve accurate implementation of the intervention" (CJAA Committee 2010, p. 1). Quality assurance and improvement is achieved through two main forms of training: (1) "ongoing consultation, feedback, and training"; and (2) "assess[ing] therapists' level of competent program delivery" (Drake 2008, p. 9). The quality assurance and improvement plans for each of the evidence-based programs are highly detailed in their processes and robust in their principles (CJAA Committee 2010; Hayes 2011, 2012).

In the early 2000s, WSIPP initiated an outcome evaluation to determine if the four evidence-based programs in operation at the time (i.e., MST, FFT, ART, COS) were working in "Washington's 'real world' setting." It found that the programs were effective in reducing recidivism so long as they were delivered in accordance with the program's model (Barnoski 2004b). This led to the Legislature directing the Institute to "develop adherence and outcome standards to ensure quality implementation of research-based juvenile justice programs" (Washington State Institute for Public Policy 2010a, p. 2). The establishment of an oversight committee, the training of qualified providers, and measuring outcomes are among the key standards that programs need to follow. With some differences in structure, rigorous and detailed quality assurance plans exist for all of the funded evidence-based programs in the state (Phelps 2011). ART and FFT, for example, employ similar structures, which include three components: (1) a quality assurance steering committee; (2) a statewide quality assurance expert; and (3) regional consultants (Washington State Institute for Public Policy 2010a, p. 2). Quality assurance is also important in the use of the risk assessment tool used by the juvenile courts (Barnoski 2004a).

7.2.7 Oversight

As noted above, under the auspices of the Community Juvenile Accountability Act, a committee was established and charged with oversight of all facets of the state's evidence-based initiative in the juvenile courts. Known as the CJAA committee, it is comprised of all of the key stakeholders in the initiative. Members represent: juvenile court administrators (representing each region); Washington State Superior Court Judges' Association Family and Juvenile Law Committee; probation and case management staff and assessment specialists; program quality assurance specialists; Juvenile Rehabilitation Administration; and the Administrative Office of the Courts. The WSIPP serves as a consultant to the committee (Washington State Institute for Public Policy 2010a, p. 2).

Until recently there was no sustained effort at transparency and accountability for the combined system of assessment and delivery of evidence-based programming. However, beginning in 2008, with a grant from the John D. and Catherine T. MacArthur Foundation, the Washington State Center for Court Research has built a system that can describe the characteristics—in terms of criminogenic needs and demographics—of juveniles entering probation, the type and duration of intervention received by them during probation, and their response to the intervention in terms of behavior, attitudes, and long-term recidivism. The Center for Court Research is currently working to improve data collection for the quality assurance components of the evidence-based programs, which will enable matching

Table 7.1 Criteria used in the Washington Block Grant

Block Grant criteria	Weight (%)
At-risk population (10–17 years)	38
Participants in evidence-based programs by risk level	25
Minority population	18
Assessed risk level of juvenile court population	15
Participants in the Chemical Dependency Disposition Alternative	3
Participants in the Mental Health Disposition Alternative or Suspended Disposition Alternative	2
Total	100

Source Adapted from Washington State Institute for Public Policy (2010a, p. 4)

of treatment provider information with youth outcomes information and further hypothesis testing about provider characteristics and youth outcomes.

7.2.8 Funding

From the beginning of Washington State's evidence-based initiative in 1997 until 2009, state funding for evidence-based programs was a based on a categorical formula. In 2009, the legislature required that funding move to a block grant formula. The bill specified that "funding priorities were to be given to evidence-based programs and alternatives diverting youth from confinement at JRA" (Washington State Institute for Public Policy 2010a, p. 4). This type of funding began in 2010.

Table 7.1 shows the criteria used in block grant funding and the contribution that each criterion represents in the total formula. Importantly, one-quarter (25 %) of the block grant formula is based on placement of youth in any one of the five evidence-based programs that are currently in operation.

7.2.9 Other Initiatives

Just as there are numerous centers contributing to the research base of evidence-based practice in the state, there are other initiatives that are committed to evidence-based practice that are operating in the state. The most prominent of these is the Seattle Youth Violence Prevention Initiative, which we profile here.

7.2.9.1 Seattle Youth Violence Prevention Initiative

The Seattle Youth Violence Prevention Initiative was started in 2009, and involved targeting roughly 800 of Seattle's most at-risk youth (e.g., repeat offenders, truants). The number of youths to be served was determined based on the actual number of juvenile violence incidents experienced in the city each year. The initiative seeks to introduce structure into these juvenile's lives as well as providing services such as cognitive-behavioral therapy. Seattle took an evidence-based approach to this initiative, rigorously studying interventions that may fit their needs and then implementing them with fidelity. The city selected several programs, such as intensive case-management, anger management training, mentoring, and street outreach. The initiative is wide-ranging, involving justice system programs, school-based interventions, and more general efforts to simply occupy the time of youths after school (in which a person who has credibility on the 'street' becomes involved with the youth).

The initiative recognized that it was essential to gain community buy-in for the program to work. While the city government has invested sizeable funds ($3.8 million per year) "neighborhood networks" have been created to identify and execute action plans. Thus, in this way, the initiative follows the work of the CTC. The initiative leadership has plans to carry out a rigorous evaluation to assess if it has achieved its goals of a 50 % decrease in juvenile violence court referrals in the neighborhood networks and a 50 % reduction in violence-related suspensions in selected schools. According to the initiative's 2011 progress report, the target number of youth being served has been reached. In addition, referrals to juvenile courts for violence as well as violence-related juvenile arrests have decreased in Seattle more than in other, comparable area (SYVPI 2011).

7.2.10 Results

It is important to remember that the goal of all of this work is to reduce juvenile recidivism and admissions to juvenile institutions and to lessen the economic burden of juvenile crime in Washington State—in the form of paying for the juvenile justice system and the harms to victims. (It is also important to remember that evidence-based practice in Washington State extends to the adult criminal justice system and, while still in development, to downstream efforts of early prevention and intervention before young people come in conflict with the law.) Of course, it is not reasonable to suggest that the mere presence of evidence-based programs (no matter how effective they are) is enough to make a difference. What is needed is evidence of a sufficient reach of the programs; that is, the percentage of eligible youths who participate in the programs. Washington State can certainly claim that their programs are succeeding on this front. The latest figures suggest that between 25 and 30 % of low to high risk youth who come before the juvenile courts in the state are participating in evidence-based programs (Phelps 2011; Washington State Institute for Public Policy 2010a, p. 6). There is every reason to believe that this figure will continue to grow in the coming years.

Based on these figures and recent research that has begun to investigate this question, there is good reason to believe that evidence-based programs are making a substantial difference in the state. According to recent research by the WSIPP (Aos et al. 2011, p. 1), "results of these crime-focused efforts appear to be paying off. Relative to national rates, juvenile crime has dropped in Washington, adult criminal recidivism has declined, total crime is down, and taxpayer criminal justice costs are lower than alternative strategies would have required." The Institute also estimates that, as of late 2011, there are approximately 1,100 fewer people in prisons in the state "as a result of the cumulative effect of Washington investments in evidence-based adult, juvenile, and prevention programs" (Aos 2011, p. 14). Conservative estimates suggest that this figure could double by 2030 (Aos 2011, p. 14).

7.2.11 Lessons Learned

In a 2008 paper, Elizabeth Drake summarizes the lessons that had been learned so far in the Washington State evidence-based initiative. First, utilize research and outcome evaluations from the literature to select potential programs. Second, create an assessment tool to ensure each individual is matched to the proper program. Third, put protocols in place that monitor quality assurance and program fidelity to ensure that programs are implemented and operated correctly. Fourth, conduct cost-benefit analyses to determine if programs are worth the investment. Finally, make "people" a priority in terms of developing lasting relationships across a wide array of agencies and stakeholder institutions. As Drake aptly puts it, "people make decisions, not reports." This was evident from the buy-in and involvement of multiple stakeholders. In Washington, statewide experts, along with a statewide quality assurance steering committee were used. This demonstrates the fact that developing a culture of evidence-based practice requires the use and cooperation of a diverse range of players.

Gaining the support of the legislature is also important in obtaining funds and in disseminating findings to the appropriate agencies. As noted above, Washington's experience with evidence-based practices really became fully entrenched in the state when the legislature passed the Community Juvenile Accountability Act in 1997. This act established a committee which would determine needs and cost-beneficial programs to implement. As a result of this act, researchers, policymakers, and practitioners worked hand-in-hand to assess, implement, and evaluate programs. This is a fundamental hurdle for much criminological and criminal justice research, which is often done in a vacuum, in isolation from the real-world in which research findings must be translated (Uggen and Inderbitzen 2010).

7.3 Florida: Outsourcing EBP

In the late 1990s, the state of Florida incarcerated youth at historically high levels, at historically high cost, even as youth crime rates had crested and begun to recede statewide. More and more youth were committed to residential facilities, even when youth were not guilty of any new law violations. A 2001 report from Florida's Office of Program Policy Analysis and Government Accountability (OPPAGA) stated that, of the 9,494 youth held in state juvenile prisons, 41 % of those youth committed were incarcerated for a non-law violation of probation (VOP). *This over-incarceration of low-risk youth—and associated costs—was the key driver in the development of the Redirection project.*

7.3.1 Early Attempts to Adopt Evidence-Based Programs

Simultaneously, the Florida Department of Juvenile Justice sought to improve community-based services (i.e., as an alternative to incarceration) by contracting for research-proven, Blueprints for Violence Prevention Model® programs such as Multi-systemic Therapy (MST), a top-tier, internationally-recognized evidence-based program (for more on MST and other Blueprints programs, see http://www.colorado.edu/cspv/blueprints/). This initial foray into evidence-based programs, or EBPs, was driven in part by the department's need for community-services that could prevent future delinquent behavior, and in part by a local provider agency's (White Foundation) desire to innovate and improve their service offerings to DJJ.

The initial MST trainings were held in 1998 in Pensacola, FL, and subsequent MST programs were started over the next 2 years in Gainesville and Jacksonville by the same provider agency with DJJ funding. Although these three MST programs were piloted from 1998 to 2003, these programs achieved mediocre success and did not lead to widespread adoption in other areas of the state. In reviewing annual reports of these early implementation efforts, adherence data suggested that the programs were not implemented with full fidelity to the model as designed and therefore struggled to consistently produce meaningful outcomes. In addition, the programs faced strong opposition from local stakeholders who held a 'get tough' point of view—and as a result youth in the MST program were frequently removed from the program prematurely if any further delinquency (i.e., even low level, non—violent offending) occurred during the course of treatment.

7.3.2 Looking for Answers to Implementation Problems

After several attempts by the department to assess and address the problem, then Assistant Chief Bernie Warner contacted the MST developers to ask: *why isn't Florida getting the outcomes that are achieved in other states and systems?* The MST developers visited Florida in 2003 and assessed the state of the programs operating there at that time. Two key findings emerged from that trip: first, the MST teams operating in the state had been subjected to **reduced funding** allocations over the 5 years since the pilot programs were implemented, and the provider agency had absorbed that reduction by **terminating the training and consulting**

relationship with MST Services, the dissemination organization that supports the implementation of MST worldwide. Second, it was also learned that a second Blueprints Model program, Functional Family Therapy (FFT), had several programs operating in the state, but not serving DJJ youth and operating with very little involvement from FFT Inc., the agency that oversees FFT implementation and ensures fidelity to that model of treatment. Based on that visit, and in order to achieve better outcomes and a high 'return on investment,' Warner recommended that in future projects, DJJ:

- Adequately fund training, QA, and ongoing consultation to maintain program fidelity.
- Invest in program oversight to ensure implementation of all programs was consistent with recommended policies and practices re program implementation.
- Monitor outcomes through consistent, annual program evaluation and reporting.

7.3.3 A Legislative and Executive Partnership: The Redirection Project

In the Fall of 2002, Warner convened several meetings with the MST and FFT dissemination organizations and with OPPAGA director Gary Van Landingham in the Fall of 2002, with the idea that the programs ought to be funded as necessary to ensure high-fidelity implementation, but also to rigorously evaluate the effort to ensure a positive impact—not to just assume one. As an arm of the Florida Legislature, OPPAGA played a key role in developing (and evaluating) policies that impact funding and legislative decisions in future sessions. At the time, Van Landingham was closely following the conversations about EBPs that were occurring at the Washington State Institute for Public Policy (WSIPP), and he sought to model the FL project after the cost-effectiveness work of Steve Aos and colleagues there.

In her chapter on the implementation of evidence-based programs nationally, Sonja Schoenwald (an MST stakeholder involved in these discussions) describes the conversation and the plans to create the 'Redirection Project' that emerged in the months that followed. In 2003, the Florida Legislature undertook a statewide initiative to import evidence-based treatments for juvenile offenders and evaluate the effects of those treatments in Florida. The legislation was discharged (in 2004) through the state Department of Juvenile Justice in a new program called Redirection. Redirection only imported models whose implementation and outcomes were favorable in Washington and other states, and MST and FFT were imported… The Legislature and the Department of Juvenile Justice collaborated with the purveyors of MST (and FFT) to create the infrastructure, funding, and regulations needed to support implementation (Schoenwald 2010).

During the 2004 Session, the Florida Legislature, following the lead of Gus Barreiro, Chairman of the Criminal Justice Appropriations Committee, passed a statutory proviso that created the Redirection Project in order to provide evidence-based alternatives to commitment. That mandate included specific direc-tives to build the project around evidence-based programs such as MST and FFT. At that time, the Department assessed the resources needed to manage the project and concluded that the knowledge, experience and expertise necessary to oversee a project of this scope was not available internally to the organization but could be most effectively procured externally. In October of 2004, Evidence-Based Associates (EBA) was identified as the project management organization (i.e., General Contractor) that would oversee the project and be held accountable for ensuring that the programs were implemented with fidelity. In this arrangement, DJJ stipulates contractually the evidence-based capacity to be available in each region; the performance benchmarks; and the frequency and content of report-ing; EBA is held accountable (and pays financial penalties) whenever any con-tract benchmark is not achieved. This arrangement has been consistent for 8 years and has produced significant reductions in recidivism, in placement and in related costs (estimated at over $200 million through 2012).

In addition to the contract oversight provided by the Department of Juvenile Justice, the Redirection project was independently evaluated annually by OPPAGA from 2006 to 2010. Reports (including the most recent report, linked here) are available on line at http://www.oppaga.state.fl.us/Summary.aspx?report Num=10-38. There were a total of five evaluations completed by OPPAGA (some of which won national policy awards for their high quality), each showing positive effects for Redirection compared to similar youth placed in residential programs and significant cost-savings, before the Legislature discontinued funding for such evaluations in 2011. Youth who were enrolled in Redirection consistently achieved significant decreases (compared to matched controls who received residential treatment) in re-arrests, felony reconviction, and subsequent commitment in adult system.

7.3.4 Scaling Up Redirection: An Implementation Model

Over a 6-year period, the scope of the Redirection project successfully scaled five times (i.e., from 300 youth in 2004 to 1,500 youth at its peak in 2009). During that time, Redirection served nearly 7,000 youth and families, and saved more than $140 million in public dollars by diverting youth from residential commitment to more effective evidence-based, community-based options.

Rigorous attention to project implementation details, such as monthly case-load and quarterly staff turnover reports, ensured 'high-fidelity' implementa-tion of MST and FFT. (Note: Brief Strategic Family Therapy (BSFT), from the University of Miami, was added in 2006 as a third EBP in Redirection, based on the Blueprints designation of this model as a 'Promising' practice.)

Redirection has received Statewide recognition for efficient and effective innovations (Davis Productivity Award of Excellence, Tallahassee 2007) and national awards for implementation of scientifically-based programs (Substance

Abuse Mental Health Services Administration (SAMHSA) Science-to-Service Award, Washington, DC 2008); similarly, Redirection has been recognized by the Southern Poverty Law Center (2009), Fight Crime Invest in Kids (2008), Blueprints for Violence Prevention (San Antonio 2010), and the Annie E. Casey Foundation (Baltimore 2011) for its innovative approach to providing evidence-based services to high-risk youth involved in the juvenile justice system.

Having served as General Contractor for four different DJJ Commissioners over the first 6 years of the project, EBA experienced the need to identify and focus on key factors that contribute to success, such as:

1. The ability to attract, compete and hold accountable best-in-class Providers of evidence-based programs. Having received funding for evidence-based program delivery, EBA competitively procured subcontracts for service delivery with provider organizations. In many cases, subcontracts were won by local provider agencies but in some cases, when local providers did not appear ready, willing and able to implement a rigorous program, EBA would seek known providers outside the state to encourage participation in the bidding process.
2. The ability to monitor and evaluate subcontractor performance and, when performance did not meet specific standards, to develop corrective actions to address performance deficits. EBA traditionally works to support a provider to achieve goals over a 6–12 month corrective action period, but will not renew subcontracts and will rebid services when warranted.
3. Based on existing strong relationships with Blueprint Model programs, EBA has the ability to coordinate closely with the Program Developers to plan, train and scale a program statewide (currently in 18 of 20 of Florida's judicial circuits).
4. The ability to bridge communications throughout all court districts in the state ensuring that all stakeholders are well-informed about Redirection's progress. Stakeholders can be a significant determinants of success in many jurisdictions. Attitudes about evidence-based programs range from highly supportive ('members of the choir') to highly skeptical, and in some cases even hostile. EBA's regional program managers have the task of working with stakeholders to hear their concerns, build alignment on areas of common ground, and keep the project moving forward toward performance goals (*pete we could go on and on here—tell us what you need*).
5. Experience and expertise to successfully implement multiple gold-standard treatment models.

7.4 California: Letting it Happen

7.4.1 Overview

The Golden State found itself in the same position at about the same time as Connecticut and later Louisiana; being sued by the Department of Justice over conditions of confinement within their institutions. Rather than accept the verdict of DOJ and the many experts who had testified at numerous hearings about the ineffectiveness and lack of leadership demonstrated by the CA juvenile justice system, CA choose to litigate the matter and oppose the court appointed master at every turn.

After more than a decade of defensive wrangling the state finally decided to withdraw from the juvenile justice field almost all together, leaving county probation departments to solve the programming issues that they had been unable to, without the help of any state leadership or technical assistance. Since this new mandate to develop more effective juvenile justice programs was imposed just before the state realigned the adult criminal justice system, by requiring counties to supervise the less serious felons and parole violators who had previously been sent to prison, it is not surprising to find little EBP progress in the juvenile justice field. In all of the leading states, responsibility for juvenile corrections is completely separate from that for adult corrections, even at the local level. A few CA counties are making use of some blueprint programs but most are sticking with simpler classroom based models like CBT and ART to satisfy the demand for EBPs

California is the most populous sub-national entity in North America. If it were an independent country, California would rank 34th in population in the world. Its population is one-third larger than that of the next largest state, Texas. As of 2006, California had an estimated population of 37,172,015, more than 12 % of the U.S. population. This includes a natural increase since the last census of 1,557,112 people and an increase due to net migration of 751,419 people. Immigration resulted in a net increase of 1,415,879 people, and migration from within the U.S. produced a net increase of 564,100 people. California is the 13th fastest-growing state.

No single racial or ethnic group forms a majority of California's population, making the state a minority-majority state. Non-Hispanic whites make up 40.1 % of the population. Spanish is the state's second most spoken language. Areas with especially large Spanish speaking populations include the Los Angeles metropolitan area, the US-Mexico border counties of San Diego and Imperial, and the San Joaquin Valley. Nearly 43 % of California residents speak a language other than English at home, a proportion far higher than any other state [6].

Per capita GDP in 2007 was $38,956, ranking eleventh in the nation. Per capita income varies widely by geographic region and profession. The Central Valley is the most impoverished, with migrant farm workers making less than minimum wage. Recently, the San Joaquin Valley was characterized as one of the most economically depressed regions in the U.S., on par with Appalachia. Many coastal cities include some of the wealthiest per-capita areas in the U.S. The high-technology sectors in Northern California, specifically Silicon Valley, in Santa Clara and San Mateo counties, have emerged from the economic downturn caused by the dot-com bust. In 2010, there were more than 663,000 millionaires in the state, more than any other state in the nation.

7.4.2 *Juvenile Justice in California*

California is a decentralized state in which local County Probation Departments handle all juveniles and adult offenders, with the exception of those committed to state facilities. In recent years the Juvenile Division of the Department of Corrections and Rehabilitation (formerly the California Youth Authority), housed as many as 9,000 juveniles and young adults. In recent years that number has fallen below 1,000 as the counties were restricted from sending all but the most serious offenders to the state (Krisberg et al. 2010).

In 2006 there were 232,000 juvenile arrests in CA. Eighty percent were referred to probation departments. Probation departments filed petitions in one-half of those cases, and the juvenile courts granted 62 % of the petitions (64,500). While California's rate of juvenile arrests (5,357 per 100,000 ages 10–17) is below the national rate (6,603), California has the nation's highest rate of juvenile offenders in local custody—3.82 per 1,000 youth aged 12 to 17—twice the national rate (State Commission on Juvenile Justice 2009, pp. 24–26). One contributing factor appears to be the recent increase in juvenile arrests for violent felonies: between 2004 and 2008, the number of these arrests increased by 13 % and the rate increased every year except for a slight decline in 2008. By contrast, the number and rate of adult arrests for violent felonies fell during this period according to the California Department of Justice.

7.4.3 *An Extra Long Exploration Phase*

In the language of Implementation Science, the exploration phase of implementation is when policy makers and stakeholders come together to explore their options and make decisions. In 2001 the Little Hoover Commission faulted the state for failing to provide leadership, coordination and oversight to the variety of juvenile justice efforts taking place at the local level. Their recommendations included:

- Making prevention the primary policy for reducing youth crime and violence.
- Creating the organizational infrastructure to define goals, establish strategies and implement programs.

Neither of these recommendations was followed by the state.

The Little Hoover Commission took up the cause of juvenile justice again in 2008 with its report: Juvenile Justice Reform: *Realigning Responsibilities* (Report #192, July 2008). Youth advocates told the Commission that the most serious threat to successful realignment was the lack of a leadership structure at the state level to guide and oversee the juvenile justice system. Witnesses also were quick to point out that the weak leadership structure was not new. Youth advocates, the Commission and others had identified this unusual structural void numerous times over the past two decades.

7.4.4 Evidence Based Programming for Juveniles in California

Over the past 8 years the Juvenile Justice and Crime Prevention Act (JJCPA) has provided more than 100 million per year for counties to implement "community-based programs that have proved effective in reducing crime and delinquency among at-risk youth and young offenders". The level of required proof is very low. With the notable exception of the few Blueprint model programs supported by these funds, not a single one of these programs has been able to "prove" its effectiveness with the kind of rigorous evaluation methods that would lead others to agree with the finding. This is why California programs for juvenile offender do not end up on any of the "what works" or "best practice" lists.

California places tens of thousands of juveniles into the justice system every year and has the nation's highest rate of juveniles in local custody. This experience generally leaves these offenders with the same, and sometimes higher, rates of recidivism. Evidence-based programs (EBPs) are one of the few potential antidotes for this unintended outcome.

At one time California was considered on the cutting edge of juvenile corrections. The California Youth Authority and its ability to maintain supervision of youthful offenders until age 25 were thought to be the model for the future. Research conducted by the CYA's own team of psychologists in the 1960s appeared to demonstrate that their community based treatment model reduced recidivism rates substantially, until another researcher reviewed their work and showed that the reduced recidivism rate was due to greater leniency on the part of community treatment parole officers rather than any change in the youths' behavior. Following the demise of the CYA research efforts, California juvenile justice programming fell under the influence of the "nothing works" philosophy attributed to Robert Martinson, focusing on sanctions instead to control the population.

It was not until a new wave of juvenile violence appeared in the mid 1990s that there was increasing interest in youth violence prevention. The Surgeon General and the Centers for Disease Control (CDC) took on youth violence as a leading health risk. The California Wellness Foundation launched an ambitious program to develop community based violence prevention programs. However, without any serious commitment to program evaluation, the more than 100 million invested by the foundation in youth violence prevention activities failed to produce a single reliable model of violence prevention that other communities could use (Greenwood et al. 2001)

In 2006 there were 232,000 juvenile arrests (State Commission on Juvenile Justice 2009). Eighty percent were referred to probation departments. The departments filed ward ship petitions in one-half of those cases, and the juvenile courts granted 62 % of the petitions (64,500). While California's rate of juvenile arrests (5,357 per 100,000 ages 10–17) is below the national rate (6,603) (Office of Juvenile Justice and Delinquency Prevention 2010), California has the nation's highest rate of juvenile offenders in local custody—3.82 per 1,000 youth aged

12 to 17—twice the national rate (State Commission on Juvenile Justice 2009, pp. 24–26). One contributing factor appears to be the recent increase in juvenile arrests for violent felonies: between 2004 and 2008, the number of these arrests increased by 13 % and the rate increased every year except for a slight decline in 2008 (California Department of Justice 2010). By contrast, the number and rate of adult arrests for violent felonies fell during this period (California Department of Justice 2010).

That so many juveniles are in the justice system and in custody does not bode well for public safety. Several strands of research strongly suggest that confinement of juveniles results in no appreciable reduction of subsequent delinquent behavior and often increases it (Lipsey and Cullen 2007). Perhaps more troubling, researchers have found that routine "rehabilitative" programs generally produce a negligible reduction in recidivism and sometimes cause an increase (Lipsey 1999). Finally, a recent meta-analysis concluded that juveniles who are processed into the juvenile justice system, rather than diverted, experience increased recidivism (except for first-time offenders) (Petrosino et al. 2010).

In 2001 the Little Hoover Commission published its report on youth violence prevention, Never to Early, Never to Late: To Prevent Youth crime and Violence. The commission faulted the state for failing to provide leadership, coordination and oversight to the variety of efforts taking place at the local level. Their recommendations included:

- Making prevention the primary policy for reducing youth crime and violence.
- Creating the organizational infrastructure to define goals, establish strategies and implement programs.

Neither of these recommendations was followed by the state.

In its first cut at realignment in 2007, the state transferred responsibility to the counties for all but the most serious youth offenders, saving millions of dollars. The counties had long supervised the vast majority of youth involved in the juvenile justice system, but up until the realignment, they had flexibility in choosing which offenders they sent to state facilities. Under realignment, the state has codified which offenders can be sent to the state. The realignment also dedicated new funding from the savings to counties to establish and expand programs and services for the shifted youth offender population.

Through this historic policy change, policy-makers could have chosen to create or designate an existing government department or committee to lead and oversee the realignment to ensure that a continuum of effective juvenile justice responses is available statewide. Policy-makers opted instead for a largely "hands off" approach.

The Little Hoover Commission took up the cause of juvenile justice again 2008 with its report: Juvenile Justice Reform: Realigning Responsibilities (Report #192, July 2008). Youth advocates told the Commission that the most serious threat to successful realignment was the lack of a leadership structure at the state level to guide and oversee the juvenile justice system.

Witnesses also were quick to point out that the weak leadership structure was not new. Youth advocates, the Commission and others had identified this unusual structural void numerous times over the past two decades. Three recommendations by the Commission attempted to deal with this problem:

- To improve public safety and provide statewide leadership on juvenile justice policy, the governor and the Legislature must consolidate programs and services into a streamlined Governor's Office of Juvenile Justice outside of the California Department of Corrections and Rehabilitation, to develop a strategy for a comprehensive, statewide juvenile justice system that includes a complete and consistent continuum of evidence-based services for youth and to oversee county programs funded by state General Fund allocations.
- Require the Division of Juvenile Justice Policy, consisting of positions shifted from the California Department of Corrections and Rehabilitation, including officials from the Divisions of Juvenile Facilities, Programs and Parole, to:
  - Provide leadership, technical assistance and guidance to help counties implement and expand evidence-based programs for juvenile offenders to improve outcomes, to set priorities for filling identified gaps and to lead and guide counties in developing regional consortiums and regional juvenile offender facilities.
  - Conduct research and analysis on best practices and provide a Web-based information clearinghouse.
  - Coordinate with other state entities that have a role in providing youth services, including the departments of mental health, alcohol and drug programs, social services and education, and provide guidance to counties on opportunities to leverage funding sources.

- Require the Division of Juvenile Justice Planning and Programs, with positions shifted from the Corrections Standards Authority Planning and Programs Division, to:

  - Oversee county juvenile offender programs funded through annual state General Fund allocations to ensure that evidence based programs are implemented.
  - Oversee and analyze county outcome reports and provide an annual report on juvenile justice performance measures to the governor and the Legislature.

None of these reforms, which were enacted in most of our leading states, was enacted in CA. The State's continuing failure to provide strong leadership and oversight of county programs, including the development of the data reporting infrastructure that would make real oversight possible, has left juvenile programming at the local level hamstrung by this neglect.

The Juvenile Justice and Crime Prevention Act (JJCPA) has provided more than 100 million per year for counties to implement evidence based programs over the past 8 years. More than a billion dollars invested by California in programs that "allegedly" have been shown to work. However, with the notable exception of the few Blueprint model programs supported by these funds, not a single one of these programs has been able to demonstrate its true effectiveness with the kind of rigorous evaluation methods that would lead others to agree with the finding. This is why California programs for juvenile offender do not end up on any of the "what works" of 'best practice' lists.

For most outcomes, counties assess their progress by comparing the results for participating minors and a reference group (i.e., participants prior to entering the program, prior program participants, juveniles comparable to those who received program services, or some other external reference group). The length and timing of the evaluation periods vary from program to program. For example, one program might compare the arrest rate of participants for the 3-month period prior to program entry with their arrest rate during the first 3 months of the program, whereas another program might use a longer time period and compare the arrest rate prior to program entry with the arrest rate following program exit. These weak evaluation standards make it impossible to judge the effectiveness of programs with any degree of confidence.

In 2004 the $137 million in JJCPA funding covered 187 programs that served 106,055 youth or about $1,300 per youth. This amount is enough to support some serious programs for a large number of youth. In 2010 the 126 million in JJCPA funds was used to support 166 programs. If just half of those funds had been invested in one of the proven Blueprint model programs such as MST, at approximately $5,000 per case, it could have provided cost-effective programing for some 12,600 youth, which would have reduce crime and future corrections costs. Since each MST team of four therapists can handle about 100 youth per year, it would take approximately 126 MST teams to provide this service. In 2001 California had only 11 MST teams.

Several county probation departments have been able to tap into technical assistance and training provided by the California Institute for Mental health (CIMH) in developing their EPBs. In 2001 The CiMH Center for Child and Family Services launched its first efforts to support the availability of services based upon practices that have strong research support. This effort evolved into the CiMH Values-Driven Evidence-Based Practices Initiative, designed to increase the availability of mental health practices supported by research—evidence-based practices—and is guided by the following principles:

- Consumers, family members, service providers, managers, administrators and all members of our communities should have information regarding the effectiveness of particular mental health practices to assure fully informed decision making.
- The adoption of new practices must take into account many significant priorities unique to its context; however, it should prioritize consumer and family choice, cultural competency, and practices with scientific research supporting their effectiveness. Community, agency, and personal values must guide the process of selecting to implement and/or participate in an evidence-based practice.
- Effective implementation processes, which adequately support practitioners, managers, and administrators, are key to improving quality of practices offered to consumers of mental health services.

CIMH's Caring for Foster Youth Project published the report *Evidence-based Practices in Mental Health Services for Foster Youth* in March 2002. This report, which was supported by the Zellerbach Family Foundation, outlined and organized the best research information available at the time, regarding the mental health needs of children in foster care as well as the state of research in the area of mental health services for this population. There is virtually a complete overlap in the needs of foster care youth, who are at high risk for delinquency, and actual delinquents themselves.

As a result of interest in applying the information contained in the monograph, the CiMH Center for Child and Family Services and Cathie Wright Center initiated the Juvenile Justice & Child Welfare Technical Assistance Project. Supported by The California Endowment, California Wellness Foundation, and the Zellerbach Family Foundation, this project approached Children's Systems of Care across the state, beginning the first implementations of Multidimensional Treatment Foster Care (MTFC) in California, and the first cohort of Functional Family Therapy (FFT) sites.

Learning from these early experiences, CIMH refined its approach to supporting model adherent establishment of practices, resulting in the Community Development Team (CDT) Model for implementation. CiMH/CWTAC partnered with the University of Washington to train the first cohort of Incredible Years (IY) BASIC Parenting Facilitators in 2004. Ensuing support from the Walter S. Johnson Foundation to improve juvenile justice mental health programming with the adoption of Teaching Prosocial Skills (TPS), as well as interest in cognitive behavioral therapies such as the Depression Treatment Quality Improvement (DTQI) model and Trauma-Focused CBT (TF CBT). DMH supported MHSA training sponsored the first CiMH High Fidelity Wraparound Project implementation in California. in 2006. And in 2006 through a contract with the Los Angeles County Department of Mental Health, CIMH is assisting with the multisite implementation of Multi-Systemic Therapy (MST), FFT, MTFC, IY, and TF CBT.

Despite these efforts California still continues to lag behind many other states in its rate of adoption for the best EBPs. It is not as if there are no probation officials in California who do not know what has to be dome to expand the use of high quality EBPs. It is just that there is no one individual or entity with the mission of connecting the dots and bringing these various pieces of expertise together. CIMH provides an excellent example of the roles an Evidence Based Center (EBC0 can play. However the CIMH development effort is limited in resources. In order to expand the availability of EBPs for Probation youth, it seems apparent that it needs much more access to EBP training and assistance than it is currently receiving from CIMH.

A more detailed look at the availability of EBP programs in CA is provided by Fig. 7.10, which shows the availability of programs by county. The counties with the most programs per capita tend to be counties with small populations such as Humbolt, Sutter and Mendecino. Sacramento and Los Angeles Counties are the only two counties that have fielded all three of the proven Blueprint programs for juvenile offenders. Many of the largest counties are limited to a small number of just one or two of the best Blueprint models.

Availability of proven family
interventions in CA

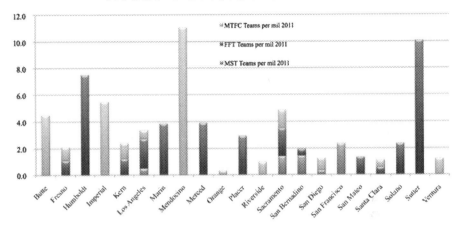

Fig. 7.10 Availability of proven family intervention programs in California (per 100,000 population)

7.4.5 *The Future*

The latest big development in CA criminal justice was the passage of "realignment" legislation last year, requiring counties to handle most non-violent offenders who used to go to prison, as well as most probation and parole violators (http://www.calrealignment.org/, Krisberg and Taylor-Nicholson 2011). This means that since October of 2011, most County Probation Departments have been struggling to realign their resources and either identify or develop new programs that will be appropriate for this new adult offender population. The problem is that there was very little training and guidance to the people developing the plans, and no assistance with implementation. As a result, most CA probation departments are likely to be struggling with program selection and fidelity issues in regard to adult programs for some time, before they turn to the special case of juveniles. Recall that in all of the states that lead in the use of EBPs, the administration of juvenile programs is completely separate from programs for adults.

Chapter 8
Lessons for Potential Champions in Other States

Evidence-based practice in delinquency prevention has come a long way in the past 15 years. This progress has been aided by the development, documentation, and dissemination of a number proven program models by university-based development teams and the efforts of a number of organizations and individual researchers to provide authoritative and up-to-date lists of those programs that appear to be effective, not to mention the strength of the evidence supporting this judgment. Some of this progress can also be attributed to the application of cost-benefit models with findings showing that substantial monetary benefits can accrue to the government and taxpayers in the short-term. Nothing captures the attention of a politician or policymaker quite like a government program that pays for itself. Leaders in state and local government across the country have also played some role in championing evidence-based practice, ushering in a possible new era that values "getting smart" on crime over "getting tough".

There is good cause for concern about the rate at which legitimate evidence-based programs are being implemented. In juvenile justice, it is estimated that only about 5 % of youth who should be eligible for evidence-based programs participate in one (Hennigan et al. 2007). While those few states that have looked carefully at their needs now provide more than ten teams of therapists per every 100,000 of their population that are delivering the three top delinquency prevention models (FFT, MST, MTFC), most states provide less than two teams per 100,000.

One reason for this low utilization rate for EBPs is the general lack of accountability for performance within the juvenile justice and community corrections systems, or even any ability to measure outcomes. Only rarely does a jurisdiction take delinquency prevention and intervention seriously enough to measure the outcome of its efforts. Without performance measurement, the only reason for serious concern about a local juvenile program is when some scandal hits the papers or the Federal Government steps in.

There are many other challenges that can impede the adoption of new EBPs at the local level. Some still dismiss the EBP movement as just another fad. Others are able to convince themselves that their current programs are evidence-based and

P. Greenwood, *Evidence-Based Practice in Juvenile Justice*, 101
SpringerBriefs in Translational Criminology, DOI: 10.1007/978-1-4614-8908-5_8,
© The Author(s) 2014

do not need to be displaced. Others are not able to afford the up-front staffing and training costs associated with launch a new program.

Finally, shifting to the use of an evidence-based program raises a whole host of concerns that may not have been experienced in the past. The close monitoring of fidelity and method of providing supervision and feedback are likely to be new experiences for staff and supervisors. The accountability built into every step of the process will also be new.

State governments are a vital link to advancing evidence-based practice and ensuring that efforts at the local level can flourish. Our research has identified five states that clearly lead all others in promoting evidence-based practice in delinquency prevention. Case studies of these states show a modest yet growing investment in a number of evidence-based programs, including FFT, MST, and MTFC. Their experiences offer a number of lessons for policymakers, practitioners, and advocates for youth in other states.

8.1 Summary of Findings

All of our five leading states, and many of the other top performers, entered the exploration phase and began looking at EBPs because they were seriously dissatisfied with the quality of their existing programs, particularly the perceived overuse of residential placements. In New Mexico and Maine there were concerns that many of the youths being sent to placements did not belong there and could be treated in the community. In Connecticut there were concerns about scandalous conditions in their juvenile facilities and over-reliance on incarceration. In Louisiana interest in EBPs began with concerns about the quality of medical and behavioral health in juvenile institutions, which eventually led to concern about programs in the community.

During their exploration phase all of our leading states took the opportunity to develop their own local expertise. Specific individuals were given the task of reviewing the "what works" literature and visiting sites that had already adopted models of interest. They also took the time to recruit and involve key stakeholders who would be required to assist with statewide implementation while sharing their expertise with local communities.

For most of the leading states the installation phase involved: arranging for training from the model purveyor; selecting the site(s) for pilot testing; and training of affected personnel.

Initial implementation was usually in pilot sites selected to provide a realistic local test of the selected model. It was usually during this pilot test period that states established or created formal relationships with some Institute or Center for Excellence which would serve as the evaluator for the pilot and technical expert, technical assistance provider, and quality assurance monitor as models moved to scale. In all the leading states, statewide support began with a single EBP (MST) with support for additional models added over time.

8.2 Seven Lessons

The following seven lessons are distilled from this study which: Identifies five states that far in front of all the others in making proven Blueprint Model Programs, that have been demonstrated to be cost-effective in reducing violence and delinquency, available to the high-risk youth and families that could benefit from them:

(1) The expansion of EBPs throughout a state does not happen by accident. All of the leading states were actively involved in facilitating and directing the expansion of EBPs, as are those on the next level down as well.

(2) Juvenile EBPs are separate and much more advanced than community corrections EBPs for adults. In all of the leading states responsibility for juvenile programming was completely independent and separate from the adult system.

(3) As we have already learned from research on implementation science and Communities That Care, pulling together a collaborative group, representing all the key stakeholders, as early in the process as possible, particularly when it comes to identifying community needs and program options, appears to be a critical early step.

(4) Empirical assessment of client needs and current program capability inevitably leads to an evidence based approach to looking for new programs to better meet the needs of their community.

(5) Completion of the two previous steps, and many others, is greatly facilitated by the establishment of an Institute or Center for Best Practice that can provide friendly technical assistance to counties and ensure a steady stream of reporting to stakeholders on how their programs are performing. These intermediary Centers are the primary source of guidance and support for local practitioners, and their primary contact with the research community.

(6) It will take any state two or more years to move through the process of statewide expansion, proceeding from early exploration to achieving desired outcomes on a statewide basis. Many states may require a year or more to reach the pilot testing phase (by improving data systems, staffing, etc.), another 2 years to get the pilot test right, and additional years to expand programs across the state.

(7) The last lesson 7 concerns the value of adopting proven model programs from Blueprints rather than relying on programs identified by less reliable rating systems. The ability of these programs to consistently perform above expectations is one of the factors that convinced local policymakers to continue moving toward evidence-based practice. Failure is not an option.

Any jurisdiction will have its hands full for at least a year after implementing a new evidence-based program. There is a steep learning curve. Any organization identified as a resource center for evidence-based practice has to start by identifying a fairly small list of proven programs it is prepared to support. Developing expertise with several new evidence-based programs, all at the same time, is difficult and not recommended. Additional programs can be added to the list over time, as demand requires.

With a growing knowledge base, state and local governments should be optimistic about the potential of evidence-based practice to prove its value in delinquency and mental health prevention and intervention. Drawing upon the lessons learned in the leading states, remaining open minded to new evaluation findings and the needs of communities will go a long way toward addressing the need for greater accountability, effectiveness, efficiency, and sustainability in how we deal with young people who come in conflict with the law.

References

Alexander, J. F., Pugh, C., Parsons, B. V., & Sexton, T. L. (2000). Functional family therapy. In D.S. Elliott & C. O. Boulder (Eds.), *Blueprints for violence prevention* (*Book 3*) (2d ed.). University of Colorado: Center for the Study and Prevention of Violence, Institute of Behavioral Science.

Andrews, D. A., & Dowden, C. (2006). Risk principle of case classification in correctional treatment: A meta-analytic investigation. *International Journal of Offender Therapy and Comparative Criminology, 50*, 88–100.

Alexander, J. F., & Sexton, T. L. (2002). Functional family therapy: A model for treating high-risk, acting-out youth. In F. W. Kaslow (Ed.), *Comprehensive handbook of psychotherapy: Integrative/eclectic* (Vol. 4, pp. 111–132). Hoboken, NJ: Wiley.

Aos, S. (2011). *Updates and new findings: Crime trends in washington & policy options that reduce crime and save money.* Paper presented at Senate Human Services and Corrections Committee, December 8, 2011.

Aos, S, Lee, S., Drake, Elizabeth K., Pennucci, A., Klima, T., Miller, Marna G., et al. (2011). *Return on investment: Evidence-based options to improve statewide outcomes—July 2011 Update.* Olympia: Washington State Institute for Public Policy.

Barnoski, R. (2004a). *Assessing risk for re-offense: Validating the Washington State juvenile court assessment.* Olympia: Washington State Institute for Public Policy.

Barnoski, R. (2004b). *Outcome evaluation of Washington state's research-based programs for juvenile offenders.* Olympia: Washington State Institute for Public Policy.

Billings, J. R., & Cowley, S. (1995). Approaches to community needs assessment: A literature review. *Journal of Advanced Nursing, 22*, 721–730.

Brunelle, J. (1980). *The Maine almanac.* Extract. Available at http://www.mainehistory.info/history.html

Bumbarger, B. (2011). Presentation at Pennsylvania Juvenile Court Judges Conference, Harrisburg, PA.

Bumbarger, B. K. (2012). Interview with Peter W. Greenwood, April 2012.

Bumbarger, B. K. (2012). Presentation at Blueprints Conference, San Antonio, Texas, April 2012.

Bumbarger, B. K., & Campbell, E. M. (2011). A state agency-university partnership for translational research and the dissemination of evidence-based prevention and intervention. *Administration and Policy in Mental Health and Mental Health Services Research.* doi:10.1007/s10488-011-0372-x.

Bumbarger, B.K., Moore, J., & Rhodes, B. (2010). Impact of evidence-based interventions on delinquency placement rates. Presentation at 2011 Society for Prevention Research annual meeting.

Bumbarger, B., & Perkins, D. (2008). After randomized trials: Issues related to dissemination of evidence-based interventions. *Journal of Children's Services, 3*(2), 53–61.

P. Greenwood, *Evidence-Based Practice in Juvenile Justice,*
SpringerBriefs in Translational Criminology, DOI: 10.1007/978-1-4614-8908-5,
© The Author(s) 2014

Bumbarger, B., Perkins, D., & Greenberg, M. (2009). Taking effective prevention to scale. In B. Doll, W. Pfohl, & J. Yoon (Eds.), *Handbook of youth prevention science*. New York: Routledge.

Bumbarger, B. K., & Perkins, D. F. (2008). After randomised trials: Issues related to dissemination of evidence-based interventions. *Journal of Children's Services, 3*(2), 53–61.

Bumbarger, B. K., Perkins, D. F., & Greenberg, M. T. (2010). Taking effective prevention to scale. In B. Doll, W. Pfohl, & J. Yoon (Eds.), *Handbook of youth prevention science* (pp. 433–444). New York: Routledge.

Bureau of Labor Statistics (2011). Washington. Available at http://www.bls.gov/eag/eag.wa.htm

California Department of Corrections and Rehabilitation (2012). Corrections Standards Authority, Juvenile Justice Crime Prevention Act Annual Report, March 2012.

Campbell, D. T. (1969). Reforms as experiments. *American Psychologist, 24*, 409–429.

Chamberlain, P., & Reid, J. B. (1998). Comparison of two community alternatives to incarceration for chronic juvenile offenders. *Journal of Consulting and Clinical Psychology, 66*, 624–633.

Children Youth and Planning Board 2011 Annual Report 2 Judicial District: 16th Judicial District (http://www.justice.gov/crt/about/spl/documents/lajuvfind1.php

Chorpita, B. F., Daleiden, E. L., & Weisz, J. R. (2005). Modularity in the design and application of therapeutic interventions. *Applied & Preventive Psychology, 11*(2005), 141–156.

Chorpita, B. F., Becker, K. D., & Daleiden, E. L. (2007). Understanding the common elements of evidence based practice: Misconceptions and clinical examples. *Journal of the American Academy of Child and Adolescent Psychiatry, 46*, 649

Chorpita, B. F., & Regan, J. (2009). Dissemination of effective mental health treatment procedures: Maximizing the return on a significant investment. *Behaviour Research and Therapy, 47*, 990–993.

Cinquemani, C. (2011). Maine by the numbers compares state rankings in key indicators. *Maine Heritage Policy Center*. Available at http://www.mainepolicy.org/2011/06/maine-by-the-numbers-compares-state-rankings-in-key-indicators/

City-Data. (2010). *Connecticut-economy*. Available at http://www.city-data.com/states/Connecticut-Economy.html

Cohen, J., Mannarino, A. P., & Deblinger, E. (2006). *Treating trauma and traumatic grief in children and adolescents*. New York: The Guilford Press.

Colgan, C., & Barringer, R. (2007). Brief history of Maine rural development policy. In D. Vail & L. Pohlmann (Eds.). *Health care and tourism: A lead sector strategy for rural Maine*. MECEP. Available online at http://www.mecep.org/SpreadingProsperity.asp

Commonwealth of Pennsylvania (2010). *Juvenile court justice commission: History*. http://www.jcjc.state.pa.us/portal/server.pt/community/about_jcjc/5984

DePrato, D. K. (2012). Juvenile justice system reform and public health: The impact of louisiana models for change. IPHJ Handout May, 2012.pdf.

Daleiden, E. L., Chorpita, B. F., Donkervoet, C. M., Arensdorf, A. A., & Brogan, M. (2006). Getting better at getting them better: Health outcomes and evidence-based practice within a system of care. Data Trends, April No. 132 http://datatrends.fmhi.usf.edu/summary_132.pdf

Davis, C., Human Service Collaborative (2007). *Developing a therapeutic support service*. Farmington, CT: Child Health and Development Institute of Connecticut, Connecticut Center for Effective Practice.

Dore, M. M., Aseltine, R., Franks, R. P., & Schultz, M. (2006). *Endangered youth: A report on suicide among adolescents involved with the child welfare and juvenile justice systems*. Farmington, CT: Child Health and Development Institute, Connecticut Center for Effective Practice.

Dorsey, C. (2012a). Interview with Michael Rocque, February 1, 2012.

Dorsey, C. (2012b). *Organizational capacity statement of the Maine SAC*. Muskie School of Public Service.

Drake, E. (2008). *Lessons learned in Washington state: implementing and sustaining evidence-based juvenile justice programs*. Paper presented at Minnesota Juvenile Justice Forum, June 19, 2008.

Drake, E. K., Aos, S., & Miller, M. G. (2009). Evidence-based public policy options to reduce crime and criminal justice costs: Implications for Washington State. *Victims and Offenders, 4,* 170–196.

Elliot, D. S. (1997). *Blueprints for violence prevention.* Boulder: Center for the Study and Prevention of Violence, University of Colorado.

Elliott, D. S., & Mihalic, S. F. (2004). Issues in disseminating and replicating effective prevention programs. *Prevention Science, 5,* 47–52.

Farrington, D. P., & Welsh, B. C. (2006). A half-century of randomized experiments on crime and justice. In M. Tonry (Ed.), *Crime and justice: A review of research* (Vol. 34, pp. 55–132). Chicago: University of Chicago Press.

Feinberg, M. E., Jones, D., Greenberg, M. T., Osgood, D. W., & Bontempo, D. (2010). Effects of the communities That care model in pennsylvania on change in adolescent risk and problem behaviors. *Prevention Science, 11,* 163–171.

Fixsen, D. L., Blase, K. A., Naoom, S. F., & Wallace, F. (2009). Core implementation components. *Research on Social Work Practice, 19,* 531–540.

Fixsen, D., Naoom, S., Blase, K., Friedman, R., & Wallace, F. (2005). *Implementation research: A synthesis of the literature.* Tampa: University of South Florida, Louis de la Parte Florida Mental Health Institute, National Implementation Research Network (FMHI Publication #231).

Ford, J., Gregory, F., McKay, K., & Williams, J. (February 2003). *Close to home: A report on behavioral health services for children in Connecticut's juvenile justice system.* Farmington, CT: Child Health and Development Institute of Connecticut, Connecticut Center for Effective Practice.

Franks, R. P. (2010). *Role of the intermediary organization in promoting and disseminating best practices for children and youth: The Connecticut center for effective practice.* Child Health and Development Institute, September 1, 2010.

Franks, R. P., & Adnopoz, J. (2007). *Implementing evidence-based practices at the state level: Challenges, successes, and lessons learned.* 19th Annual Conference Proceedings-A System of Care for Children's Mental Health: Expanding the Research Base, pp. 45–48.

Franks, R. P., Schroeder, J. A., Connell, C. M., & Tebes, J. K. (2008). *Unlocking doors: Multisystemic therapy for Connecticut's high-risk children & youth.* Farmington, CT: Child Health and Development Institute, Connecticut Center for Effective Practice.

Glassman, J. (2011). *The state of Maine's economy.* J. P. Morgan Chase & Co. Available at https://www.chase.com/online/commercial-bank/document/Maine.pdf

Greenwood, P. W. (2006). *Changing lives: Delinquency prevention as crime-control policy.* Chicago: University of Chicago Press.

Greenwood, P. W. (2008) Prevention and intervention programs for juvenile offenders: The benefits of evidence-based practice. *Future of Children, 18*(2).

Greenwood, P. W., & Welsh, B. C. (2012) *Promoting evidence-based practice in delinquency prevention at the state level: Principles, progress, and policy directions, crime & public policy.*

Greenwood, P. W., Model, K. E., Rydell, C. P., & Chiesa, J. (1996). *Diverting children from a life of crime: Measuring costs and benefits.* Santa Monica, CA: RAND.

Greenwood, P., Wasserman, J., Flora, J., Howard, K. A., Schleicher, N., Abrahamse, A., Jacobson, P., Marshall, G., Oken, C., & Chiesa, J.(2001). *The California wellness foundation's violence prevention initiative findings from an evaluation of the first five Years.*

Greenwood, P. W., & Turner, S. (2012). Establishing effective community-based care in juvenile justice. In F. Sherman & F. Jacobs (Eds.), *Promoting health and well being in the juvenile justice system.* Wiley & Sons.

Harris, P., Lockwood, B., & Mengers, L. (2009). *A CJCA white paper: Defining and measuring recidivism* [White paper]. Retrieved from http://www.cjca.net

Hawkins, J. D. (1995). Controlling crime before its happens: Risk-focused prevention. *National Institute of Justice Journal, 229,* 10–18.

Hawkins, J. D., Catalano, R. F., Arthur, M. W., Egan, E., Brown, E. C., Abbott, R. D., et al. (2008). Testing communities that care: The rationale, design and behavioral baseline equivalence of the community youth development study. *Prevention Science, 9,* 178–190.

Hawkins, J. D., Kosterman, R., Catalano, R. F., Hill, K. G., & Abbott, R. D. (2005). Promoting positive adult functioning through social development intervention in childhood: Long-term effects from the seattle social development project. *Archives of Pediatrics and Adolescent Medicine, 159,* 25–31.

Hawkins, J. D., Welsh, B. C., & Utting, D. (2010). Preventing youth crime: Evidence and opportunities. In D. J. Smith (Ed.), *A New response to youth crime* (pp. 209–246). Cullompton, Devon, UK: Willan.

Hayes, C. J. (2011). *Washington state aggression replacement training quality assurance plan.* Unpublished report.

Hayes, C. J. (2012). Interview with Brandon C. Welsh, January 4, 2012.

Henggeler, S. W., Schoenwald, S. K., Borduin, C. M., Rowland, M. D., & Cunningham, P. B. (1998). *Multisystemic treatment of antisocial behavior in children and adolescents.* New York: Guilford.

Henggeler, S. W., & Lee, T. (2003). Multisystemic treatment of serious clinical problems. In A. Weisz (Ed.), *Evidence-based psychotherapies for children and adolescents* (pp. 301–322). New York, NY: Guilford Press.

Hennings, R. (2007). *Taking measure.* Maine Department of Corrections, Division of Juvenile Services.

Infoplease. (2011). *Connecticut.* Pearson Education, Inc. Available at http://www.infoplease.com/ipa/A0108191.html

Infoplease. (2007). *Coastline of the United States.* Pearson Education, Inc. Available at http://www.infoplease.com/ipa/A0001801.html

InfoPlease. (2005). *Pennsylvania.* Available at http://www.infoplease.com/ipa/A0108264.html

Institute of Medicine (2001). Crossing the quality chasm: A new health system for the 21st century.

Jones, D., Bumbarger, B. K., Greenberg, M. T., Greenwood, P. W., & Kyler, S. (2008). *The Economic return on pccd's investment in research-based programs: A cost-benefit assessment of delinquency prevention in pennsylvania.* University Park, PA: Evidence-based Prevention and Intervention Support Center.

Juvenile Justice Advisory Group. (2010). *State of Maine juvenile justice advisory group 2010 Annual Report.* Available at http://www.maine.gov/corrections/jjag/index.html

Juvenile Justice Task Force. (2010). *The Maine juvenile justice task force: an integrated approach to transforming Maine's juvenile justice system.* University of Southern Maine, Muskie School of Public Service.

King, E. (2012). Interview with author Michael Rocque, February 1, 2012.

Krisberg, B., Vuong, L., Hartney, C., Marchionna, S. (2010). *A new Era In California juvenile justice: Downsizing the state youth corrections system.* Berkeley, CA: Berkely Center for Criminal Justice.

Krisberg, B., & Taylor-Nicholson, E. (2011). *Realignment: A bold new era in California corrections.* Berkeley: Earl Warren Institute.

Kuklinski, M. R., Briney, J. S., David Hawkins, J., & Catalano, R. F. (2010). Cost-benefit analysis of communities that care outcomes at eighth grade. *Prevention Science.* doi:10.1007/s11121-011-0259-9.

Krzyzek, M. (2011). Youth employment in Connecticut. *The Connecticut economic digest.* 3.

Landenberger, N. A., & Lipsey, M. W. (2005). The positive effects of cognitive-behavioral programs for offenders: A meta-analysis of factors associated with effective treatment. *Journal of Experimental Criminology, 1,* 451–476.

Lee, S., Aos, S., Drake, E., Pennucci, A., Miller, M., & Anderson, L. (2012). Return on investment: Evidence-based options to improve statewide outcomes, April 2012 Update, #12-04-1201.

Lipsey, M. W. (1992). Juvenile delinquency in treatment: A meta-analytic inquiry into the variability of effects. In T. D. Cook, H. Cooper, D. S. Cordray, H. Hartmann, L. V. Hedges, R. J. Light, T. A. Louis, & F. Mosteller (Eds.), *Meta-analysis for explanation: A casebook* (pp. 83–127). New York: Russell Sage Foundation.

Lipsey, M. W. (2006). The effects of community-based group treatment for delinquency: A meta-analytic search for cross-study generalizations. In K. A. Dodge, T. J. Dishion, & J. E. Lansford (Eds.),

Deviant peer influences in programs for youth: Problems and solutions (pp. 162–184). New York: Guilford Press.

Lipsey, M. W. (2009). The primary factors that characterize effective interventions with juvenile offenders: A meta-analytic overview. *Victims and Offenders, 4,* 124–147.

Lipsey, M. W., & Cullen, F. T. (2007). The effectiveness of correctional rehabilitation: A review of systematic reviews. *Annual Review of Law and Social Science, 3,* 297–320.

Lipsey, M. W., & Howell, J. C. (2010). *Improving the effectiveness of juvenile justice programs: A new perspective.*

Little Hoover Commission (2008). *Juvenile justice reform: Realigning responsibilities* (Report #192, July 2008).

Lopez, M. E., Kreider, H., & Coffman, J. (2005). Intermediary organizations as capacity builders in family educational involvement. *Urban Education, 40,* 78–105.

Louisiana Juvenile Justice Screening, Assessment, and Treatment Services Trends 2007–2009–2011.

Louisiana Models for Change, Summary of Work: 2008–2011, LA MfC Status Report 2011.pdf.

Louisiana MfC EBP TOOL KIT for Fostering a Movement Towards Evidence-Based Screening, Assessment, and Treatment, pdf.

Maine Department of Juvenile Services. (2006). *Juvenile justice advisory group.* Available at http://www.maine.gov/corrections/jjag/index.html

Matthews, B., Hubbard, D. J., & Latessa, E. (2001). Making the next step: Using evaluability research to improve correctional programming. *The Prison Journal, 84*(4), 454–472.

Meyers, J. C. (2000). *Delivering and financing children's behavioral health services in Connecticut.* Farmington, CT: Child Health and Development Institute of Connecticut.

Meyers, J. C. (2006). Pathways to reforming children's mental health service systems: public and personal. In A. Lightburn & P. Sessions (Eds.), *Handbook of community-based clinical practice* (pp. 204–220). New York, NY: Oxford University Press.

Nstate. (2011). *Connecticut.* Nstate, LLC. Available at http://www.netstate.com/states/intro/ct_intro.htm

Miller, K. (2009). Census: Maine oldest, whitest state in nation. *Bangor daily news.* May 13, 2009. Available at http://bangordailynews.com/2009/05/13/politics/census-maine-oldest-whitest-state-in-nation/

Nalli, G., Lapping, M., & Ebersten, S. (2011). *The state government/university system partnership program briefing to joint standing committee on health and human services.*

National Advisory Mental Health Council Workgroup on Child and Adolescent Mental Health Intervention Development and Deployment (2001).

National Advisory Mental Health Council Workgroup on Services Research and Clinical Epidemiology (2006).

National Center for Juvenile Justice (2005a). *Maine: Juvenile justice state profile.* Available at http://www.ncjj.org/State/Maine.aspx

National Center for Juvenile Justice (2005b). *Pennsylvania: Delinquency services summary.* Available at http://www.ncjj.org/State/Pennsylvania.aspx

National Center for Juvenile Justice (2005c). *State juvenile justice profile: Washington.* Available at http://www.ncjj.org/State/Washington.aspx

Noreus, R. (2011). *Annual juvenile recidivism report.* University of Southern Maine, Muskie School of Public Service. Maine Statistical Analysis Center.

Noreus, R. (2012). *Recidivism rates of youth discharged from supervision 2006–2009.* University of Southern Maine, Muskie School of Public Service. Maine Department of Corrections, Division of Juvenile Services, Recidivism Report Series.

Nstate (2012). *Pennsylvania.* Available at http://NetState.com

Pennsylvania Budget and Policy Center (2011). *Poverty rises sharply in PA and the nation.* September 27, 2011. Available at http://pennbpc.org/poverty-rises-sharply-pa-and-nation

Phelps, D. (2011). Interview with author Brandon C. Welsh, December 21, 2011.

Phillippi, S. (2011). Presentation to Juvenile Justice Reform Act Implementation Commission, February 21, 2011.

Phillippi, S. (2010). Evidence Based Practice for Juvenile Justice Reform in Louisiana 2010.pdf.

Phillippi, S. Improving Services for Youth in the Juvenile Justice System: Outcomes and Implementation Strategies from Louisiana Models for Change in Juvenile Justice Reform (draft).

Prentky, R., & Righthand, S. (2003). *Juvenile sex offender assessment protocol-II (J-SOAP-II) manual*. NCJ 202316.

Rhoades, B. L., Bumbarger, B. K., & Moore, J. E. (2012). The role of a state-level prevention support system in promoting high-quality implementation and sustainability of evidence-based programs. *American Journal of Community Psychology*. doi:10.1007/s10464-012-9502-1.

Righthand, S. (2012). Interview with Michael Rocque, January 19, 2012.

Righthand, S., & Welch, C. (2001). *Juveniles who have sexually offended: A review of the professional literature*. OJJDP.

Righthand, S., Welch, C., Carpenter, E. M., Young, G. S., & Scoular, R. J. (2001). *Sex offending by Maine youth: Their offenses and characteristics*. Report to the Maine State Legislature. Available at http://www.maine.gov/dhhs/ocfs/cw/caan.html

Rooks, D. (1996). Prospects for reform in Maine's department of corrections. In *Maine choices 1997: A preview of state budget issues*. Augusta, Maine: Maine Center for Economic Policy.

Rubin, M. (2012). Interview with author Michael Rocque, February 1, 2012.

Rubin, M., Dodge, J., Noreus, R., & Rocque, M. (2009). *Maine Crime & Justice Data Book*. Muskie School of Public Service: University of Southern Maine.

SAMHSA. (2007). *Trauma affect regulation: Guide for education and therapy (TARGET)*. Available at http://nrepp.samhsa.gov/ViewIntervention.aspx?id=104

Schoenwald, S. K. (2010). From policy pinball to purposeful partnership. In J. R. Weisz & A. E. Kazdin (Eds.), *Evidence-based psychotherapies for children and adolescents* (2nd ed., pp. 538–553). New York: Guilford Press.

Schwalbe, C. S. (2007). Risk assessment for juvenile justice: A meta-analysis. *Law and Human Behavior, 31*, 449–462.

Scott, E. S., & Steinberg, L. (2008). *Rethinking Juvenile Justice*. Boston, MA: Harvard University Press.

Seattle Youth Violence Prevention Initiative. (2011). *Safe youth, safe community: A progress report*. Available at http://www.seattle.gov/neighborhoods/education/youthInitiative/documents/SYVPI-2011ProgressReportlowres.pdf

Sherman, L. W., Gottfredson, D. C., MacKenzie, D. L., Eck, J. E., Reuter, P., & Bushway, S. D. (1997). *Preventing crime: What works, what doesn't, what's promising*. Washington, DC: National Institute of Justice, U.S. Department of Justice.

Stelk, W., & Slaton, E. (2010). The role of infrastructure in the transformation of child-adolescent mental health systems. *Administration and Policy in Mental Health and Mental Health Services Research, 37*, 100–110.

Stoodley, B. (2012). Interview with Michael Rocque, March 13, 2012.

Tapley, L. (2011). Reducing solitary confinement. Exclusive interview: How Maine's corrections commissioner dropped supermax numbers by 70 percent and became a national leader in prison reform (if anybody follows). *The Portland Phoenix*. November 2, 2011.

Tay, L. (2005). *Attachment and recovery: Caring for substance affected families*.
Farmington, CT. Child Health and Development Institute, Connecticut Center for Effective Practice.

Uggen, C., & Inderbitzin, M. (2010). Public Criminologies. *Criminology and Public Policy, 9*, 725–749.

Vanderploeg, J. J., Bracey, J. R., & Franks, R. P. (May 2010). *Strengthening the foundation: Analysis of Connecticut's outpatient mental health system for children*. Farmington, CT: Child Health and Development Institute, Connecticut Center for Effective Practice.

Vanderploeg, J. J., Franks, R. P., Plant, R., Cloud, M., & Tebes, J. K. (2009). *Extended day treatment: A comprehensive model of after school behavioral health services for youth*.

Vanderploeg, J. J., & Meyers, J. C. (2009). *The intensive in-home services decision tree: A framework for decision-making in Connecticut*. Farmington, CT: Child Health and Development Institute, Connecticut Center for Effective Practice.

Vanderploeg, J. J., Schroeder, J. A., & Franks, R. P. (November 2007). *Emergency mobile psychiatric services: Recommendations for model enhancement*. Farmington, CT: Child Health and Development Institute, Connecticut Center for Effective Practice.

Viljoen, J. L., Mordell, S., & Beneteau, J. L. (2012). *Prediction of adolescent sexual reoffending: A meta-analysis of the J-SOAP-II, ERASOR, J-SORRAT-II, and Static-99*. Law and Human Behavior. Online First. doi: 10.1037/h0093938

Washington State Institute for Public Policy (1998). *Watching the bottom line cost-effective interventions for reducing crime in Washington*. Olympia: WSIPP.

Washington State Institute for Public Policy (2010a). *Washington state juvenile court funding: Applying research in a public policy setting*. Olympia: WSIPP.

Washington State Institute for Public Policy (2010b). *WSIPP's benefit-cost tool for states: Examining policy options in sentencing and corrections*. Olympia: WSIPP.

Weisburd, D., Lum, C. M., & Petrosino, A. (2001). Does research design affect study outcomes in criminal justice? *Annals of the American Academy of Political and Social Science, 578*, 50–70.

Welsh, B. C., & Farrington, D. P. (2011). Evidence-based crime policy. In M. Tonry (Ed.), *The Oxford handbook of crime and criminal justice* (pp. 60–92). New York: Oxford University Press.

Welsh, B. C., Sullivan, C. J., & Olds, D. L. (2010). When early crime prevention goes to scale: A new look at the evidence. *Prevention Science, 11*, 115–125.

Williams, J., Ford, J., Wolpaw, J., & Pearson, G. (August 2005). *Not just child's play: The role of behavioral health screening and assessment in the Connecticut juvenile justice system*. Farmington, CT: Child Health and Development Institute, Connecticut Center for Effective Practice.

Williams, J., Franks, R. P., & Dore, M. (May 2008). *The Connecticut juvenile justice system: A guide for youth and families*. Farmington, CT: Child Health and Development Institute, Connecticut Center for Effective Practice.

Wirschem, M. (2011). Interview with Brandon C. Welsh, December 20, 2011.

Yeager, C. (2011). Interview with Peter W. Greenwood, 2011.

Index